Please return or renew this item before the latest date shown below

Thank you for using your library

STRATEGY
GENIUS

40 insights
from the
science of
strategic thinking

RICHARD A D JONES

ABOUT THE AUTHOR

Richard Jones is a consultant and entrepreneur who works on complex strategic and technology issues – developing and implementing new strategies and business models from the USA to Kazakhstan and from the Arctic Circle down to South Africa. Client work includes Shell, BT, Nike, BCG, Santander, RBS, Boots, Vodafone, Siemens and Johnson & Johnson.

The technology consultancy he co-founded (venturateam.com) is considered a leader in next generation telecoms and it has also bootstrapped its own successful operator in the highly competitive Swedish telecoms market – serving 155,000 subscribers and being ranked number 4 in the world for broadband service value prior to a sale to TeliaSonera.

He has founded or helped several other start-ups achieve returns of 40 to 75 times for shareholders. He has applied these skills to helping develop new business units for companies like BT.

The latest venture, founded with his colleagues, is taking the open access Fibre to the Home (FTTH) elements of the Swedish operation global – with the first client delivering what is believed to be the first gigabit, triple play services for subscribers in the whole of Africa.

He is very active across a number of disruptive technology areas – mobile Internet, FTTH and cloud – including as Chairman of the Smart Cities – Operations and Applications Committee for the FTTH Council MENA. Richard regularly chairs a number of technology conferences across Europe and MENA covering cutting-edge telecoms, smart cities and technology. He also delivers keynote speeches on strategy and disruption for companies like NBC/Universal.

Richard is the author of several books, including *Project Management Survival* (also available in Chinese, Polish and Latvian) and *The One Day MBA* – a book on the different skills required by executives who want to gain experience fast.

He has a degree in electronics, a masters equivalent in engineering, an MBA with distinction from the University of Warwick and is also studying for a doctorate in the strategy of technology companies.

If you'd like to get in touch Richard can be contacted at richard@venturateam.com

ACKNOWLEDGEMENTS

I would like to thank the nice people at Hodder & Stoughton for asking me to write the book and their help in editing it. Strategy is such an important topic but so badly understood. It's been a pleasure working with Iain, Alison and the others to deliver a book that I hope will help companies create and execute better strategies.

I also want to thank Stefan Stanislawski and Mikael Sandberg, my partners within Ventura Team (venturateam.com). We're into our 15th year of the adventure and have delivered strategy, business modelling, change management and implementation projects around the world together. I think it's rare to find people you really like and respect that you can work with, but I'm lucky as they are two of the best.

Finally, thanks to my lovely wife Julie and Harry and Will for the support, love and laughter, as well as allowing me the time to write this book.

PERMISSIONS

'Richard Jones is, for a broadcaster like me, on the fast dial for comment about almost everything. I am, like most of my breed, lazy and a skimmer. Richard always places the context and arrows the opinion. So this is so appropriate – genius conflated into something you can understand. A bit like Richard, really.'

Michael Wilson – Director of Business and
Economics Editor, Arise Global Networks

'Good strategic thinking is often preached; here are some good questions and frameworks for practitioners.'

Peter Davidson, FREng – Formerly Senior Innovation
Advisor to the Department for Business, Enterprise and
Regulatory Reform (BERR) and Department for
Innovation, Universities and Skills (DIUS)

'Strategy is one of those topics that many people talk about without having much idea what they mean. Richard Jones is one of the exceptions. His latest book gets straight to the point and you can see that this is someone who not only understands the topic and can explain it well, but has actually done these things and put into practice the stuff he talks about. A very good book; I recommend it strongly.'

Peter Hiscocks – CEO Judge Business School
Executive Education, University of Cambridge

First published in Great Britain in 2015 by Hodder & Stoughton. An Hachette UK company.

First published in US in 2015 by Quercus US.

British Library Cataloguing in Publication Data: a catalogue record for this title is available from the British Library.

Library of Congress Catalog Card Number: on file.

Paperback ISBN 978 1 47360 538 1

eBook ISBN 978 1 47360 539 8

1

Typeset by Cenveo® Publisher Services.

Printed and bound in Great Britain by CPI Group (UK) Ltd., Croydon CR0 4YY

John Murray Learning policy is to use papers that are natural, renewable and recyclable products and made from wood grown in sustainable forests. The logging and manufacturing processes are expected to conform to the environmental regulations of the country of origin.

Hodder & Stoughton Ltd
Carmelite House
50 Victoria Embankment
London EC4Y 0DZ
www.hodder.co.uk

CONTENTS

INTRODUCTION

Chances are your company's strategy is broken... or you haven't actually got one.

In a world that changes faster and faster, the survival of a company relies on creating and executing an effective strategy. The truth is that many companies are not asking the big questions they need to face in order to survive. Don't believe that? Fifty-seven companies stayed in the Fortune 100 for the 20 years to 1990. Only 26 managed to survive the next 20 years. Bottom line: it's harder to survive and ultra-competitive market conditions mean businesses need to make better strategic decisions.

The scary fact is that most businesses don't have a coherent strategy. That seems a ridiculous statement doesn't it? So let's explore that further. First question is to you then. Can you describe your company's strategy? Take a moment and think about what you would tell someone. I've asked this question to more than 2,500 executives.

The most popular answer is, 'we're working on a new one'. The follow-up question asking them to describe the 'old one' is, more often than not, met with a blank stare.

The second most common answer tends to be a rambling description of a PowerPoint® presentation where the person struggles to remember even the main pillars of the strategy.

Okay, you've had a chance to think about your familiarity with your company's strategy – let's look at this in more detail.

If your answer is something like 'increase revenues', then can you show me a company on the planet with the strategy to reduce revenue? I thought not, but several people have expressed that as their company's strategy! Now you're not alone in this.

If your answer is along the lines of 'people first' or 'progress through ideas' (again real responses I've received), then I'd respectfully suggest that you have a strapline not a strategy.

If the 'strategy' is 'to increase sales by 5 per cent year on year' then you don't have a strategy – you have a rolling budget. This is perhaps the biggest sin in strategy as you are essentially creating expectations for this year based on what happened last year. It's like driving a car only looking in the rear view mirror. If the road bends or there is some unexpected obstacle then you're going to have a nasty surprise.

Let's assume that you have something that is more thought out than some of the real examples above. Time for the hard question. Alongside the fine words about conquering new territories, refreshing product ranges or indeed whatever has been defined, is there any mention of how these objectives will be achieved? The reason this is important is that if the 'how' has not been considered, there is a chance the strategy itself is unachievable. I'm not saying this is definitely the case, but again I've seen plenty of audacious strategies that have been defined without sufficient thought to how they might be delivered.

Now it's true that the job of the organization is to execute strategy but some thought about the 'how' must have taken place or you risk having unrealistic expectations and an organization that is going to struggle to deliver. Execution may require short-term actions to re-deploy staff, increase some activities while reducing others. There may be mergers or acquisitions needed. In the longer term, the underlying skills and capabilities may need to evolve to match changes in the business environment and/or new areas to be exploited. If the challenges, costs and impact, etc. of doing these have not been factored into creation of the strategy then the risk of failure is multiplied exponentially. The problem is then that the strategy looks great on paper or projected in the board room but the failure to consider the bottom-up execution is hidden. The problem only becomes obvious when the company fails to progress as expected, or lurches into trouble.

Classic strategic thinking is flawed

Some of the classic strategic approaches are not exactly dead but they certainly have been struggling to deliver the right answers in times of significant change. Royal Bank of Scotland, Kodak, Polaroid, Saab, General Motors, Chrysler, Jessops, Blockbuster (and an ever-growing list of household names) didn't veer towards bankruptcy through a lack of intellectual horsepower. It happened because they failed to position themselves correctly for the changing circumstances around them.

Strategy is for every manager

The strategy of an organization should be felt at every level. Think about this. If someone in the guts of an organization doesn't understand the overall strategy then how can you expect them to work in a way that is consistent with it? There will be some parts of the strategy that are more sensitive/secret but if your company is trying to build high-quality cars (e.g. Volkswagen) then someone running a plant to get the maximum number of cars out of a factory, regardless of their quality, is doing the wrong thing!

Wherever you are in an organization your job is to understand (and challenge where appropriate) strategic objectives imposed on you and create a coherent strategy for how your piece of the jigsaw will deliver what is required. The only difference over time is that the scope of what you are managing will increase.

If you're lucky then you'll also be part of the larger scale strategic discussions. This can allow you to really make a difference (as well as it being incredibly satisfying).

The rest of this book will help guide you through a little of the classic thinking but also a huge amount of cutting-edge thinking about how to formulate and execute strategy.

ABOUT THIS BOOK

This book is laid out so that each chapter can be read as a standalone piece. However, the chapters are structured with a logical flow to take you through the different steps in the journey of formulating and executing strategy. It is not exhaustive in that certain areas will not be covered in detail as they are already well understood by most business people. However, the book will mention these to signpost some of the other important parts to the discrete steps in formulating the strategy.

Why companies are deluding themselves about strategy

This looks at how companies are failing to develop and share effective strategies – instead basing their direction on straplines and/or rolling targets of the types discussed earlier. A chapter also looks at the problem of strategies not being communicated down through the organization.

What should strategy be?

This section looks at what a strategy should contain, the balance between 'me too' and real stretch objectives and finally how you focus the whole organization around a strategy.

What goes wrong?

In this section, the chapters cover some of the classic ways that businesses are destroyed. It looks at the dangers of success, where a company like Kodak is doing so well it becomes a serious challenge to recognize and accept the need for significant change. Especially if this change will sacrifice revenues. It also talks about disruptive technologies and the way they frequently allow established players to become de-positioned by new entrants.

Disruption and how to survive it

With the accelerating impact of new technologies, this section looks deeper at what disruption is and what it means for companies. It then goes on to consider how to not just survive the impact of technology or business model disruption, but actually exploit it.

Understanding competitive advantage

Developing a sustainable competitive advantage has been a cornerstone of business strategy for some time and it is clearly a highly desirable position to achieve. This section will look at the classic but still important thinking in this area and then move on with discussing how the concept of a sustainable advantage stands up in today's turbulent times.

Understanding the situation

The first step in developing strategy is to understand the current and likely future environment and situation for the company. This will cover a classic model for understanding the competitive environment before considering a modern twist on this approach and then a chapter on identifying when a business model is running into trouble.

Creating strategy

This part includes chapters that introduce some unusual concepts into the development of strategy – covering areas such as learning from failure as well as tools to help understand the changing environment. It will consider business models and business model innovation in detail.

Developing strategic alternatives

This section includes a number of chapters that range from simple thoughts on how to develop and then evaluate potential strategic alternatives.

Driving innovation

This section considers not just optional ways to innovate but has chapters considering how much innovation is optimum as well as how to best configure an organization to be innovative.

Executing and embedding strategy

There are chapters on how to help embed strategy through clear communications through to setting up the right metrics that align with the desired strategy. The final chapter is an example of an end-to-end approach for developing strategy.

1 **DO YOU HAVE A GOOD STRATEGY?**

How companies are often deluding themselves about the quality and even existence of their strategy

Okay so of course you have a strategy in your company. You heard it at a conference and it was about … erm … well …Well someone knows what it is and hopefully it's correct and everyone is somehow magically following it.

The shocking and sad point to note is that in far too many companies, there is no appropriate strategy.

Richard Rumelt believes that many organizations, when asked about their strategy, are actually doing lots of 'look-busy, doorknob polishing'. You should read his book just to read phrases like that but he's identifying how organizations can delude themselves by doing lots of things that may ultimately be inconsequential or even take them in the wrong direction. His view is based on looking at strategies from an academic as well as practical perspective – always with blistering honesty as he tries to set deluded CEOs and even the US government on the right path.

He believes that if you don't actually identify the challenges and obstacles that you are really facing as part of the strategy process, you are likely to end up with a stretch goal, a modified version of last year's budget or a wishlist (probably without any definition of how you're going to achieve this last one). This is a 'Phantom Strategy'. Everything seems fine. There is a strategy document. It looks like it might be a strategy as it has some nice long words in it and the PowerPoint slides have some nice images. You might even have been assisted with its creation by some consultants or others who should know better. But at the end of all this, although you have something that looks real, it's actually the proverbial chocolate teapot. Roughly the right shape but totally useless.

Beyond that, the secondary concern is that the existence of the Phantom Strategy means you stop paying attention to a question you think you've answered but haven't.

The rolling budget masquerading as a real strategy is surprisingly common. The strategy process in some companies has declined into a simple summation of the performance forecasts of individual business units that are then added together. The next step is often a killer of any ambition to deliver a 'real' strategy. Someone at the heart of the organization looks at the numbers, decides the total is a bit low and then seemingly arbitrarily adds some extra onto the figures.

After a few years of this happening you'll find many business unit teams will just send in figures they've barely thought about but which show an increase on the previous year's budget. They are fully expecting someone to pump the figures up later so keep their 'opening bid' deliberately low. Sound familiar? Depressing isn't it?

At the other end of the scale of cluelessness is a strategy with some big, hairy, audacious targets and absolutely no idea about how to get there.

Back to Rumelt for a second. He discusses the reason why bad strategy is so common and it's pretty sobering.

The first point is that senior managers are trained to implement top-level goals set by other people but are less familiar with choosing between the different paths that exist in taking a company forward strategically. So this leads to either poor choices or a simple failure to choose. With a finite set of resources, trying to pursue too many avenues is not a great idea.

A second factor is where strategy becomes secondary when a charismatic leader is in place. Leadership is not strategy. Historical precedents might show how one person can inspire people to do the extraordinary but it's probably better to combine the great leader with the best strategy rather than only having the former.

Where such a leader is not present, the other extreme is the template-based, strategic process. This can be useful and certainly should help discover some useful insights but that style is not always appropriate.

Roger L. Martin adds some ideas into the mix – underlining the problem of strategies that are actually just rolling budgets but also expanding on this to suggest that this problem comes from a focus on strategic planning functions. Thinking about strategic planning leads to an emphasis on costs, which naturally leads to becoming inward looking and budget focused..

Although a management team may genuinely wish to produce a good strategy, their selection of a particular framework may force them into a pattern of thinking that focuses on what is within the control of the organization. Henry Mintzberg introduced the phrase 'emergent strategy' to illustrate how the results reached in an organization are not purely about the deliberate results of a strategy. Things happen around the firm that will blow it off the course it sets and Mintzberg coined the term, in part to try to get managers to recognize this fact. Otherwise, they can simply start to believe that they are fully in control of everything. That's a dangerous delusion.

SIGNS THAT YOU DON'T HAVE A REAL STRATEGY

Rumelt's nothing if not practical. He provides a few interesting questions to ask to help you see if your organization is suffering from having a Phantom Strategy.

The presence of fluff

That means long words and endless steams of nouns designed to make the author look intelligent and erudite. However, it's often no more than window dressing. I dislike those types of phrases in strategies anyway, as the objective is to pass on what may be a very complicated concept in a simple way. Long, complicated sentences and obscure words won't help.

No defined challenges

If the strategy document doesn't address the challenges facing the organization then you run the risk of them being missed and/or you won't be able to manage them.

Goals dressed up as strategy

If the strategy has missed the challenges that need to be faced, the chances are it will contain goals but little in the way of how they will be achieved. It's wishful thinking rather than a thought-through plan of action to take on the challenges.

> ### Case study
>
> One media agency I worked with talked about its strategy being to beat its competitors by 50 per cent. When pressed, it became clear the success or otherwise could only be measured at the end of the year rather than en route, month by month. The team didn't know if it referred to customers, revenues, margins, accounts won, retention or anything tangible. Yet they were happily working away thinking they had a strategy.

If you want to pick a strategy document apart on this particular issue, then simply ask what needs to happen for the organization to meet its overall objectives. If that question isn't answered in the strategy documentation then you definitely have problems.

Poor strategic objectives

The objectives are things you have to achieve but they are poor if they don't address key issues and/or cannot be achieved.

So what are the big takeaways here?

- Look at what you're doing and how you're doing it. If your strategy is a rolling budget or based on closed assumptions about things continuing as they always have been, re-vamp the process to give yourselves the real vision and intelligence you need.

- Keep focused on asking yourself and the team 'what is going on here?' It's an oft-repeated phrase in this book but a crucial question to ask. Get to the bottom of why things are as they are – not simply the apparent reasoning at the surface. This should help you move on to understanding what has to happen for the company to achieve the aims of this strategy?
- You need to be vigilant for indicators that you're heading for trouble. Actively look for the warning signs. Look out for complacency. Look out for copy-paste strategy or rolling budget mentalities. If you don't, the organization (particularly one in a very competitive environment) is likely to struggle.

Sources

Martin, Roger L., 'The Big Lie of Strategy Planning', *Harvard Business Review*, January 2014

Mintzberg, H. & Waters. J. A. (1985), 'Of Strategies, Deliberate and Emergent', *Strategic Management Journal*, Vol. 6 Issue 3 (Jul/Sept 1985) pp 257–72

Rumelt, Richard, *Good Strategy/Bad Strategy* (Profile Books, London, 2012)

See also

Chapter 2 –Takes a different view of this question and asks if there is a shared view on strategy across the organization

Chapter 3 – Has a look at a definition

In addition there are 37 more chapters to paint a broad picture about what strategy should be and how you should think about it.

Further reading

There are some other good books on strategy that give a background on the 'classic' definitions and thinking. They are worth a read – but they don't necessarily fix this problem of these rolling budget type approaches. If people are deluding themselves about the reality of their budget then a book isn't going to fix that easily – unless you drop it on their foot to wake them up!

Johnson, Gerry, Scholes, Kevan & Whittington, Richard, *Exploring Corporate Strategy* (FT/Prentice Hall, Harlow, 2007)

Porter, Michael E., *Competitive Strategy: Techniques for Analyzing Industries and Competitors* (The Free Press, New York, 2004)

2 CAN YOUR PEOPLE SAY WHAT YOUR STRATEGY IS?

What are they going to follow if they can't?

I've mentioned most employees' inability to articulate the strategy in their own organization. That's pretty serious, so you'd think that a short pithy summary would be pretty helpful. What I do sometimes hear quoted as the strategy in a company is sometimes short but is generally wrong. Sometimes it's a strapline like 'people first' and sometimes it's the mission statement. Sadly, having a mission statement doesn't mean it's correct, relevant, appropriate, etc. They are often externally focused, marketing statements that don't contain enough meat to actually use as the basis for developing strategy. On other occasions, the mission statement is so similar to other players in the industry you wonder how the company can create any differentiation for itself.

In their work on this topic, Collis and Rukstad discussed the concept of a meaningful 35-word strategy statement. That may be 20 seconds' worth if you were saying it. So you can't accuse them of being overlong!

They emphasized that a key aspect of strategy should be about how you are going to compete. In other words, what are you doing that is different to the competition?

In the absence of this, it is hard to know if a particular initiative is aligned with the strategy and management should be surprised if they don't get the results they expect.

The two authors described how the marketing-friendly wording in a mission statement does not constitute a strategic objective.

The latter is the thing that will help orient the company and drive it forward in the medium term. Mission statements traditionally have to placate stakeholders and customers alike – often ending up saying similar things from company to company in the same sector.

They proposed three steps in the process of creating a strategic objective to cover the objective, scope and advantage. Let's look at these in more detail.

Define the objective

This means a well-defined objective (specific, measurable, etc.) that explains what you are going to do to deliver whatever your high-level mission suggests. If the bottom line is about delivering shareholder value then what objective will do that? That's the question to be answered at this point.

Define the scope

It's easy to go down the rabbit hole of every potentially profitable area but business is about the correct application of a finite set of resources. That means what you are going to do and what you will not. Scope may cover customer types, products, services, geographies and other dimensions of what's in play, and what isn't.

Define the advantage

Of most importance is explaining why customers will buy your product/service. If you can't answer this then you need to go back and keep going back until you can. Other chapters in the book will go into this in more depth, and will describe some alternative ways of defining your advantage, but answering this question is non-negotiable.

Collis and Rukstad's view was that you could answer all this in 35 words. That might seem unrealistic but I think the point is that you have to really think hard to capture the essence of your strategy in so few words, and thinking hard is what is required. Also, 35 words are easy to pass on and for people to remember.

The company should look at changes in both customer needs and their competitor's capabilities and offerings, in order to find the 'Sweet Spot'. The Sweet Spot is the area that intersects what your customers want and what your company can do, but is **outside** the capabilities of the competition.

UNDERSTANDING YOUR COMPANY'S OWN STRATEGY

I regularly ask groups of senior executives if they can explain their company's strategy. The results are consistently disappointing.

The most common answer is: 'We're working on a new one.' I counter by asking what the old one is then and there is that instant flash of regret that they said anything at all.

The second most common answer is to start on a slightly rambling recollection of a presentation given by the CEO a while ago. People can often remember that there were five key areas or maybe it was seven. They can also normally name one or two of the areas. 'Customers… Cash…' However, they then tend to run out of steam.

The worst ever was a group of regional managing directors in a large financial services company who had met with the new CEO the previous week for a motivational session about the new direction. I asked if they were now happy they understood the strategy. Everyone nodded unconvincingly but one person very honestly and bravely shook his head. He explained that he'd heard what was said but didn't actually understand it. The CEO used words including 'nexus', 'corollary' and 'codicil', and had left the regional MD confused. He was by no means unintelligent but the CEO's use of language had hidden the actual strategy in a blur of wonderful but slightly impenetrable English.

If you like, this is the second mortal sin of strategy. The first is not having a good, executable strategy. If we assume that you have a great strategy, then the failure to communicate it clearly through the organization begs the simple question.

'If nobody knows what the strategy is, how do you expect people to act in line with it?'

In larger organizations, we'll assume the overall strategy may be correct but if it's not understood lower down in the organization it amounts to the same thing as not having a strategy. There has to be an effective waterfall or cascade effect that means business units and groups within the organization understand the overall strategy (or the part that is relevant to them). If not, well good luck!

As a final point, remember that people are mostly driven by how they are measured and rewarded. You could have the best strategy in the world but if the metrics of how someone earns a bonus (or simply keeps their job) are wrong, you will get the wrong result. People will chase the money or simply seek survival in the organization as a higher priority than thinking of following the strategy.

The only solution that is acceptable for long-term success is the right strategy, understood throughout the company and with consistent measures on individuals and groups driving what they do. If any of the three elements is missing – you've got trouble!

So what are the big takeaways here?

- **Confront the reality that people in your organization probably don't get strategy.** If you want to shock yourself, and I can pretty much guarantee you won't like the answers, ask a few people in the organization what they think the company strategy is. Does your team understand the strategy? Does the strategy express how they are going to compete in the future? Does the strategy show how we will outperform the competition?
- **Check if the strategic direction is aligned to the metrics.** At the same time, ask how their own performance, or the performance of their team, is measured. Look for the mismatches between strategy and metrics, as well as whether the strategy is understood deep into the company.

- **Just because it's hard to find a strong strategic position doesn't excuse you from looking.** Now you won't always be able to identify real 'clear blue water' where you can deliver to customer needs and the competitors cannot, but you absolutely should look.

Source

Collis, David J. & Rukstad, Michael G., 'Can You Say What Your Strategy Is?', *Harvard Business Review*, April 2008

See also

Introduction and Chapter 1 – Read them to understand why a clear and widely understood strategy is important. If nobody knows what it is or, worse still, there isn't a real strategy, then you're asking for trouble.

3 SO WHAT IS STRATEGY AND WHAT SHOULD IT DELIVER?

Defining the journey for your organization

Chapters 1 and 2 looked at why businesses sometimes confuse themselves by not having a real strategy or by failing to commit to it clearly. This chapter aims to outline a little about what strategy should be.

So let's start with something pretty basic – survival! You want the right strategy to help your organization survive and grow.

There are lots of people who have written on this topic but it's hard to get past two great thinkers in this area. Michael Porter simply stands head and shoulders above others in his contribution to business thinking and the development of models that make the complex seem simple. Richard Rumelt is perhaps the ultimate straight talker on strategy. His frustration at bad strategy literally leaps off the pages of his books.

So what have these two, and maybe a few others, to say about what makes a good strategy?

Kenichi Ohmae suggested that only by combining thinking about customers, competition and the corporation (3 C's model) could this sustained competitive advantage be found. However, the pace of technological change in some sectors means the ability to sustain advantage may be a concept that is disappearing. But that doesn't mean you shouldn't look for competitive advantage. If you ever explained to someone that your company was deliberately not searching for one (or more) then that would truly sound insane.

Porter will tell you that strategic positioning aims to find a position of sustainable competitive advantage – through either doing different things to the competition or doing the same things but in a different (and presumably better) way.

Porter combines ideas to give a three-part recipe for strategic positioning.

First – find the unique position for your company, based on:

- a small set of products to many customer types (Michelin just makes tyres but does so for the full range of vehicles that use tyres from mopeds to aircraft)
- delivery of a wide range of products/services to a tightly focused group (private banks serve the full set of financial needs but for high net worth individuals only)
- the wide range of needs of significant numbers of customers but only in a narrow segment (e.g. targeting villages and small towns only).

Second – decide what you'll not do. For example, Black & Decker is great at making small electric motors but it might struggle to create an electric toothbrush line. Its brand is simply not appropriate in trying to enter the dental hygiene market.

Third – you're looking for a great fit between what you do and the whole set of processes, metrics, skills, structure, etc. of the organization. If the fit is weak then you risk not accruing the full benefit of the activities. The risk is that someone better aligned with what they do could come in and do a better job.

Richard Rumelt's *Good Strategy/Bad Strategy* is a great read. It matches concerns I have had for many years but puts them in a very clear way. It deconstructs the history of a number of companies to consider how they have addressed the future (or not).

He starts by defining the components of a good strategy and it's well worthwhile looking at these ideas in more detail.

The first step is that a good strategy has to face up to the real challenges the company is facing and come up with a way of overcoming them. It must be cohesive in that it should have a consistent interpretation and direction coming from the analyses, evaluation and formulation of scenarios to respond to the challenge faced by the business. It is not just good because it is based on current strengths; it is also good because it is completely integrated and consistent across the organization.

A good strategy will also be actionable immediately. In other words, what you do is also defined in delivering the strategy.

The key element is that the strategy defines how the company or organization is going to address current and future challenges.

At its heart, a strategy should have a diagnosis (explaining where you are and what is happening around you now and into the future), a guiding policy and coherent action. You could paraphrase that as 'where are we?', 'what are we going to do?' and 'how are we going to do it?'.

The guiding policy is markedly different from many organizations' vision statements as they tend to be all about the destination whereas guiding policy is all about the 'how' of the journey. It is a means of addressing the current situation but should also rule out some of the potential actions the organization could take. The right strategy will deliver what Rumelt refers to as leverage – combining:

- anticipation of changes in buyer needs and competitive reactions
- concerted and focused application of effort across the organization.

WHAT SHOULD A BUSINESS STRATEGY DELIVER?

There are plenty of definitions of strategy that you can find but I've written this one to try to combine a number of different elements you'll encounter as you read through the book.

'Strategy is a plan covering the right duration for the particular industry situation, which defines and shapes the objectives of an organization – matching resources to the expectations and needs of customers, the market environment and stakeholders.'

This definition of strategy includes a number of important points. Let's break the statement down into smaller chunks and look at each piece to understand why they are so important.

Strategy provides the direction set for a given time period

Defining a strategy should give an organization a clear understanding of the direction it has chosen to follow. This strategy should be appropriate and actionable within the organization over the right period of time for the industry. You'll read more about understanding why you need the right duration for a strategy in Chapter 20.

Strategy is a blueprint

The strategy acts as the blueprint that the organization uses to decide how it operates and what it does. This ranges from setting major objectives down to defining individual tasks that are appropriate, effective and consistent with the desired direction. The strategy therefore needs to be sufficiently detailed, clear and unambiguous to allow this translation from words into action.

Strategy is about using resources effectively

Both market leaders and those challenging them need to marshal their forces very carefully. Market leaders typically have higher volumes, which provide the opportunity to benefit from economies of scale, which should in turn give them better profit margins.

Rumelt talks about the idea of a 'proximate' objective for strategy. This is one that the organization should be able to achieve, if not control. At this point, it is important to understand that the 'big objective' only makes sense if the obstacles along the way are understood clearly.

Rumelt suggested a few steps for better creation of strategy but perhaps the key was to switch focus from what is being done to why it is being done. Identifying the challenges, limits and opportunities out there will help understand the context for strategy choices far better than getting caught up in thinking about actions.

As you develop better options for the future, it is also important to eliminate any existing options by showing their limitations, inconsistencies or errors. Rumelt calls this 'create-destroy'.

So what are the big takeaways here?

- **Read the rest of the book.** Sounds strange? Well this chapter is a taster to the different elements but it's merely a taster. Tuck into the other chapters and think about the sometimes subtle aspects of strategy they discuss. Understand the full set of concepts that will enable you to approach strategy in a more effective way.
- **Question strategy. Challenge it. Examine the underlying assumptions.** Is this strategy the right one to help us stick around for years to come? Are we falling for 'flavour of the month' approaches or simply pandering to shareholder needs?
- **Try to be different in the face of everyone else thinking the same.** Most companies are, to some extent, following the same classical structured approach to strategic thinking. That's neither the right answer in all cases, or likely to help you stand out from the rest if you're all thinking the same way.

The good news is that many are doing it badly, misapplying thinking or contenting themselves with a rolling budget approach to planning.

That's good news for other organizations, who can do it right and make a huge difference to their competitiveness, revenues, margins, etc.

Sources

Kenichi Ohmae *The Mind of the Strategist: The Art of Japanese Business* (McGraw-Hill, New York, 1991)

Porter, Michael E., *Competitive Strategy: Techniques for Analyzing Industries and Competitors* (The Free Press, New York, 2004)

Rumelt, Richard, *Good Strategy/Bad Strategy* (Profile Books, London, 2012)

See also

Chapter 20 – 'Matching strategy to your situation' shows different types of strategies for different business situations. That then defines the appropriate lifespan for the strategy you are putting in place. For some firms that will be a year, for others it might be a few months.

The next chapter examines the realistic level of ambition that you should aim for in your strategy.

Further reading

Mintzberg, H. & Waters. J. A. (1985), 'Of Strategies, Deliberate and Emergent', *Strategic Management Journal*, Vol. 6 Issue 3 (Jul/Sept 1985) pp 257–72

Johnson, Gerry, Scholes, Kevan & Whittington, Richard, *Exploring Corporate Strategy* (FT/Prentice Hall, Harlow, 2007)

4 THE RIGHT AMOUNT OF STRATEGIC AMBITION

Stretch the organization without breaking it

Richard Rumelt is a must-read author on strategy. There are not too many of those but I think he's often overlooked. That's a mistake. He worries about the same things I see repeatedly in strategic work in companies.

Beyond the companies that he says are deluding themselves with their limited attempts at setting a strategy, Rumelt offers up advice about setting realistic and 'proximate' strategic objectives. He discusses the idea of sensible and achievable targets for an organization.

Although Big Hairy Audacious Goals can be great, they often hide the fact that they are impossible or that the person creating them thinks they are a substitute for good management. If there is no reasonable expectation of a 'how' being found to deliver the goal, then this is management by hoping for the best. An interesting book on sales nails this thought in the title – 'Hope is not a Strategy'.

Rumelt's view from his years of research and direct work in companies is that you need a target that you can reasonably expect to hit – if not overwhelm. When considering the typical goals set in organizations, his criticism is that these still retain too much ambiguity about the hurdles that will need to be overcome. This is an intrinsic part of his view on strategy. You must define the challenges that you need to overcome.

He cites President John F. Kennedy's ambition to get a man on the Moon, and I'd pull out one part of that to illustrate Rumelt's point. In the 1960s the technology wasn't ready to get a man to the moon, so JFK's statement recognized this and then covered the approaches to resolve this challenge.

"We propose to accelerate the development of the appropriate lunar spacecraft. We propose to develop alternate liquid and solid fuel boosters, much larger than any now being developed, until certain which is superior."

The key to cascading strategy down into an organization is that it remains consistent and I'd strongly suggest must be supported by the right metrics. These top level, proximate objectives can then be devolved into smaller proximate objectives within business units.

Now this isn't an exclusive approach. You can use the Balanced Scorecard approach to strategy mapping (as discussed in more detail in Chapter 39) and take the top level proximate objective as the seed to produce objectives in financial, learning/growth, process and customer areas. The Balanced Scorecard reminds you to measure the right things across several different aspects of the company and so will work best if being derived from the right top level objective(s).

The book talks about the idea of a proximate objective for strategy. This is one that the organization should be able to achieve, if not dominate. At this point, it is important to understand that the 'big objective' only makes sense if the obstacles along the way are understood clearly.

To create value, Rumelt identifies four different approaches to increasing value:

- deepen current advantages
- broaden the reach of the advantages
- increase demand for products/services that have advantages
- isolate the source of advantage (e.g. through patents, copyrights, brand power, exclusivity, etc.). You can also continue to improve the source of advantage continually to create a moving target for others to chase.

SPOTTING MORE SIGNIFICANT DRIVERS OF CHANGE IN YOUR INDUSTRY

Now if you want to make sure you're not being under-ambitious, Rumelt discusses a number of 'Guideposts' to demonstrate potential sources of more significant change in an industry. These markers will indicate disruption for an organization that will demand effective strategic management with more challenging and loftier targets.

Guidepost 1 – Rising fixed costs

As the fixed costs rise, the potential problem is that the costs become so high that only a few companies can afford to pay. You'll have seen this in the consolidation in some industries with very high costs.

Boeing and Airbus now dominate the large airliner market (from the Boeing 737 up to the 787 and Airbus A319 to A380 respectively).

Pharmaceutical companies are spending £billions in getting a drug to market and only a limited number of major players can afford these extreme entry costs.

Guidepost 2 – Deregulation

Moving from being in a regulated industry with only one or a small number of players to being in a market free-for-all can be traumatic for the original players.

The lack of 'true' competition means a monopoly player is unlikely to be as lean or hungry as the new entrants.

Guidepost 3 – Predictable biases

These are the ways in which organizations can believe in trends or have a bias towards certain views that are not necessarily valid. For example, in times of high demand growth, you might think this is going to continue indefinitely and not recognize that the market is saturating among those who really want the product. Another example of a biased belief is that even in times of significant change, the biggest competitor(s) will remain the winners in the future.

In other words, we lose sight of the fact that some perceived wisdom and 'facts' need to be challenged in detail.

Guidepost 4 – Incumbent response

Here's a simple concept. Incumbents won't like change and will act to resist any transitions. Where the incumbents have been successful for some time, you're also facing the fact that they may have both deep pockets and a corporate ego that will drive them to make some irrational business decisions.

Guidepost 5 – Attractor states

There are 'attractive' ways in which the industry could work in a more efficient fashion and which logically would appear to be the best state for the industry. For example, many retail operations must see online delivery as the attractor state.

You should consider the existence of one or more of these guideposts as big red flags that attention is required on the strategy for the future.

Rumelt suggested a few steps for better creation of strategy but perhaps the key was to switch focus from *what* is being done to *why* it is being done. Identifying the challenges, limits and opportunities out there will help understand the context for strategy choices far better than getting caught up in thinking about actions.

As you develop options for the future, you must also eliminate some options by showing their limitations, inconsistencies or errors. Rumelt calls this 'create-destroy'.

So what are the big takeaways here?

- **Avoid crazy and unattainable targets – they do nobody any good.** You want a level of ambition that helps you respond to the current and foreseen situation for your organization. However, you also don't want to be under-ambitious in terms of the amount of change. Rumelt's guideposts can assist as one way of recognizing when things have to change. Other chapters build on this.

- **Challenge every objective you define.** Ask lots of questions. Have we carefully thought through why this objective has been set? Does it reflect our situation – what's the evidence? Does it reflect the challenges we are facing – what's the evidence?
- **It's easy to think up stupid targets – it's a lot harder to hit them.** The right level of 'stretch' for a target will provide the right answer for an organization and also can be bought into by individuals. If it seems pointlessly hard, irrelevant or the workings behind the targets set are invisible – you're inviting lots of nods from people who inside are thinking that it's actually impossible. In a 'shoot the messenger' type organization, that will mean your team may actually lie to you about their degree of buy-in rather than put their head above the parapet and tell you. Not very helpful is it?

Sources

Rumelt, Richard, *Good Strategy/Bad Strategy* (Profile Books, London, 2012)

JFK's speech to the US Congress – 25 May 1961 http://www.jfklibrary.org/Asset-Viewer/xzw1gaeeTES6khED14P1Iw.aspx

See also

Chapter 19 – Talks about recognizing when your business model is in trouble. This is another indicator of when you might want to have more ambitious thinking baked into your strategy.

Chapter 5 – The next chapter considers why getting the right strategy can be very important, even when things are apparently going well.

Further reading

Lafley, A. G. & Martin, Roger L., *Playing to Win: How Strategy Really Works* (Harvard Business Review Press, Boston, 2013)

5 WHY THINGS GOING WELL CAN BE SO DANGEROUS

How companies can fly too close to the Sun

In particular in this chapter we'll look at views on how companies need to pay attention and potentially change in challenging ways, even when times are good. It's easy to succeed when things are going well but the challenge is to change when things are going well.

Danny Miller has written on how businesses that are successful suddenly fall from grace. He rather brilliantly called it the Icarus Paradox. In the ancient Greek legend Icarus soared too close to the Sun and by forgetting the consequences of his actions and the wings that got him so high then became the cause of his demise.

Miller sees a similar pattern with organizations. Once they achieve success, the strategy that got them there can become ever more deeply embedded in the company consciousness. The idea of deviating from that winning formula becomes harder and harder, even if the underlying competitive situation is changing (and it pretty much always does).

Think about this for a second. Can you name a company that hasn't continually reinvented itself – fundamentally changing how it operates? Hard isn't it! A few may come to mind but there are thousands that didn't change and no longer exist.

Let's have a look at the death of an iconic company.

Case study: Kodak destroys itself

The camera market in the 1980s and into the 90s was dominated by big players such as Canon, Nikon, Pentax and Olympus. They made cameras where the optics and internal mechanisms were the key factors governing performance and hence influencing buyer choice.

A Kodak engineer developed the first CCD (charge-couple device) image sensor in 1975 and this technology started to appear in a significant number of cameras for the consumer market in the early part of the 90s. The cost of digital cameras reduced as economies of scale and more aggressive competition appeared in these markets and the market shifted inexorably towards digital. This change to digital from film technology helped some companies to reposition themselves while others fared badly in the transition.

Some traditional camera companies continue to thrive in the digital era, having combined their expertise in manufacturing lenses with new electronics capabilities to create a strong range across both the consumer and professional markets.

New players have entered the market, based on their experience in electronics and video camera technology. For example, Panasonic has partnered with the legendary optics company Leica to complement its strength in electronics and create a powerful presence in the non-professional digital camera market.

These examples illustrate how technology can change a market forever and even powerhouses like Kodak can crumble in the face of such radical change – moving from domination of the film and paper era to a minor position in digital and eventual withdrawal from the market in early 2012 while under bankruptcy protection.

But more importantly, it shows what happens when you try to stick to a formerly winning formula for too long.

AVOIDING THE PITFALLS

Miller has a nice classification of ideas to try to explain some of the reasons why companies can fall so badly from grace. They form a useful checklist to guard against some of the common failings. I've paraphrased these below (with a few tweaks).

- **We tend to over-state our own abilities.** That's also true for companies that can start to believe their own hype – diluting the chance they will critically question their situation.
- **We believe the initial forecasts too much.** These may be in 'sales' mode to get a project approved but we don't pay enough attention to further analysis to see how they are evolving over time.
- **Stretch targets become amalgamated into forecasts as the norm.** A stretch target is designed to challenge but let's think about the mechanics for a moment. If you consistently use numbers that can be achieved without difficulty, your forecasts will be accurate but unexciting. If you 'go big' on the numbers and aim for stretch targets across the board, you are combining results that have a much lower chance of occurring. Chances are you'll get a number somewhat below the forecast produced in this fashion. So the forecasts are mainly going to be missed. That has an important secondary effect in that you will show everyone in the organization that forecasts and targets are unrealistic and missing them is not important anyway. This last fact will be assumed as the organization will be missing targets so regularly. You want your people to believe in targets and to try to achieve them, not assume they are unrealistic and unattainable.
- **We get so engrossed in the day-to-day stuff we neglect competitor reactions.** Sometimes companies spot a bandwagon and go headlong to catch it – forgetting that others may do exactly the same thing, a fact that can negatively affect the results they have predicted.
- **Competitors will also do things we don't expect.** They'll do that for good reasons or sometimes because of stupidity or ego getting in the way of common sense. Beware of strategies that are predicated on very specific reactions from competitors.

- **We assume we can influence everything.** We can't. Strange stuff will happen, the economy will change, legislation will affect a market, customer tastes may change, etc.
- **Forecasts are moved upwards to get a project approved.** A wily company chairman once asked me how much the target revenues had been inflated above reality. That's not how I build businesses but it was clear he was very used to seeing wildly optimistic numbers presented to him ready to be knocked back down again. My approach of just providing the estimate unchanged was almost viewed with suspicion and you could imagine his management team silently taking 15 per cent off my numbers.
- **We don't change a winning formula.** Ways of working that bring you success become ingrained and even though they may become less than ideal, they will continue in their own groove unless some external stimulus provokes a change.

Think about the Kodak example mentioned previously. It pretty much owned the world of film and photographic paper, but couldn't move on. The results were, eventually, terminal.

So what are the big takeaways here?

Don't let strategic thinking be for special occasions or when trouble hits. Try to bake in processes and approaches that constantly question the status quo and challenge orthodox thinking, rather than trying to reinforce it. You'll see this approach as a recurring theme throughout the book.

Ask yourself some challenging questions. Are we getting set in our ways? How can we be the big company but still think like the little one?

Sources

Miller, Danny, *The Icarus Paradox: How Exceptional Companies Bring About Their Own Downfall* (HarperBusiness, New York, 1990)

Kodak press release – 9 February 2012
www.kodak.com/ek/US/en/Kodak_Focuses_Consumer_Business_On_More_Profitable_Growth_Opportunities.htm

'Kodak files for bankruptcy protection', Richard Waters and Tim Bradshaw. *Financial Times* – 19 January 2012 www.ft.com/cms/s/0/68054e1c-4267-11e1-93ea-00144feab49a. html#axzz1uwqGz99S)

'Kodak: From Brownie and roll film to digital disaster' James Cowling. BBC News – 20 January 2012 www.bbc.co.uk/news/business-16627167

See also

Chapter 19 – Discusses how you can potentially spot that your business model is starting to hit trouble, before it becomes obvious!

Further reading

Johnson, Spencer, *Who Moved my Cheese?* (G. P. Putnam's Sons, New York, 1998)

6 DISRUPTIVE TECHNOLOGIES

How do smart big companies get outflanked by new technology?

Nothing lasts forever. This is particularly true in business and there is a lot to learn from the demise of iconic companies and brands. However, we tend to assume that these companies have fallen from grace in the normal cut and thrust of business. We think that a traditional competitor has done a bit better, created a new product, been a little faster and generally just outperformed the market leader.

This describes the demise of many relatively stable companies in markets where serious innovation and change are harder to produce. Oil companies remain profitable as there is no significant alternative. Car companies continue from year to year, taking market share from one another in a relatively slow evolution of the market.

So how do major companies, with sometimes almost limitless resources, allow a new entrant to eat their lunch? Are they not paying attention? Are they really that stupid?

The explanation comes in groundbreaking work by Clayton Christensen on the concept of disruptive strategies and innovation. If you want an idea about how important his book *The Innovator's Dilemma* is, then I'd mention that Steve Jobs's biography by Walter Isaacson says Jobs was deeply influenced by it. If it's good enough for Steve Jobs then … well I'm not going to argue.

Let's understand the phenomenon first and then in the next chapter we'll discuss some ways that you can identify when a disruptive bullet may be coming straight at you!

Christensen looked at the disk drive industry to illustrate the changes that occur in a fast-paced market. His ideas on disruption illustrate how a sector can be completely redefined by the emergence of a new player in a market at the expense or a more established competitor. He even used the term 'missiles' to describe these disruptions as they arrive fast and with devastating effect.

Before his work one common idea was that of the 'technology mudslide'. It suggested that companies are constantly running uphill and so cannot afford to pay attention to other technologies as they will lose pace in the current area. Christensen's work undermined the technology mudslide hypothesis while creating a more detailed picture of how companies come to be leapfrogged by disruptive technologies.

Part of his concept is that a **disruptive innovation** initially drives the emergence of a new market and associated value network. Over time, this innovation then moves from the initial market to a more traditional one and displaces the formerly dominant technological approach in that traditional market.

In contrast, established businesses can be well run and develop **sustaining or established innovations** that work fine for 'business as usual' but can still hit trouble as they are de-positioned by disruptors.

So why don't major players respond to these new technologies? Let's think about major players in an established market as a new technology emerges.

The first element is that the new technology may begin below the performance level of existing technologies and so is not of interest to the established market at that point.

The second aspect is that the new market where the technology can be applied may not match the major player's organization, processes, etc. The result is that the market may simply be too small to bother with but it may also not be profitable or attractive anyway for the established player.

These factors can allow a new player to take a leadership position in the new market and also with the new technology.

So what happens over time?

Well the new entrant is coming from a market with lower margins (compared to the established market) and so may have been forced to be leaner and more efficient than companies in the established market. As the entrant moves into the established market these organizational advantages enable it to compete very effectively.

Being first into an emerging market with a disruptive technology was very beneficial for firms that did this. Those that drove into the emerging markets for disk drives earned US$1.9 billion in revenues while those that entered late struggled to only US$64.5 million.

Christensen suggests that a new business is ten times more likely to be successful if a disruptive strategy is followed rather than one that mimics the current market. To paraphrase Einstein: 'insanity is doing the same thing over and over again and expecting different results.' These successful new companies seem to be heeding those words.

PAYING ATTENTION TO DISRUPTION

Now companies do need to pay attention to their biggest competitors. They may have similar resources and, by definition, they know your customers. The only problem is that a hawk-like monitoring of the current competition has not been enough to save many companies that have been obliterated by a new entrant that has changed the rules of the game. This may be a company with inferior resources and one that begins from a base of zero market share – yet somehow it has come into the market and quickly ended up dominating it.

Case study: The smartphone disrupts multiple products

Google's Android and Apple's IOS operating systems for phones have contributed to enormous change in multiple markets through our expanding use of smartphones.

Its range of applications makes a smartphone seem like an electronic Swiss army knife – with many individual capabilities that make a specialized tool obsolete for many. Think about the simple art of navigating your way around. You arrive in an unfamiliar town and look at your phone. The GPS and use of the mobile phone network allows your phone to locate you like a GPS tracker. But unless you think in detailed coordinates that's not very useful so you get your location from, say, Google or Apple maps and your location is now displayed (making paper street maps nearly obsolete). You know where you're trying to get to and now the phone can plot your route for you whether on foot, on a bike or going by car (undermining the after-market satellite navigation market). As screens on devices get bigger, or where we choose to use a tablet, we can mount the device in the car and it does the same as the sat nav. It might even have traffic data included (such as in Google maps but not available in all sat navs) to help optimize the route to get us to our destination more quickly.

Books such as *Product Juggernauts* and *Third Generation R&D* (see below) would point to investing the right amount of time and money into a portfolio of projects to cover off alternative technology approaches and gather an appreciation of those that might work well in the future for the company. They refine the categorization of types of innovation to also define technologies that:

- will become a source of differentiation in the future (**EMERGING**)
- might create differentiation in the future (**PACING**).

However, although I'm a big believer in this type of structured approach, the danger is that the focus is on providing incremental performance improvements to satisfy customers.

Over time, the number of competitors able to meet the performance level needed, say, in terms of functionality leads to oversupply of that attribute and the basis for competition migrates to other attributes such as reliability, convenience and finally price. This means the advantage of the company may disappear as others catch up and they have failed to explore other mechanisms for delivering value to customers.

As if to underline the severity of some disruptions, Downes and Nunes use the phrase 'big-bang disruption' per https://hbr.org/2013/03/big-bang-disruption/ to describe situations where an entire product, service or even market can be destroyed as customers move to an alternative they consider 'superior'.

So what are the big takeaways here?

- **Try to find time to look ahead.** You should look for new technologies that are capable of impacting your market and use a structured process (as described in Chapter 11) to avoid being overtaken or displaced in your market. In particular, think hard and regularly about which technologies could change how your customers' needs are met in this market.
- **Peer over the horizon.** There may be no obvious technologies that are ready today but then you should ask about which technologies are on the horizon that could enter your market if they developed. What would it take for them to be competitive? How likely is it that they can bridge the gap to the point of competing effectively?
- **Pride cometh before a fall.** No company is too big, too clever or too safe to ignore the potential impact of a disruptive approach.

Sources

Christensen, Clayton M., *The Innovator's Dilemma: When New Technologies Cause Great Firms to Fail* (Harvard Business Review Press, Boston, 1997)

Christensen, Clayton M. & Raynor, Michael E., *The Innovator's Solution: Creating and Sustaining Successful Growth* (Harvard Business Review Press, Boston, 2013)

Deschamps, Jean-Philippe & Ranganath Nayak, P., *Product Juggernauts: How Companies Mobilize to Generate a Stream of Market Winners* (Harvard Business Review Press, Boston, 1995)

Roussel, Philip A., Saad, Kamal N. & Erickson, Tamara J., *Third Generation R&D: Managing the Link to Corporate Strategy* (Harvard Business Review Press, Boston, 1991)

See also

Chapters 9 and 10 – In case this chapter has been too depressing, read these chapters that talk about not only surviving disruption but even the concept of exploiting it!

Further reading

These books provide very interesting complementary reading on how to succeed in challenging markets and move into the future. If Geoffrey Moore wrote a menu it would probably be worth reading!

Moore, Geoffrey A., *Crossing the Chasm: Marketing and Selling Disruptive Products to Mainstream Customers*, 3rd Ed (Harper Business, New York, 2014)

Moore, Geoffrey A., *Escape Velocity: Free Your Company's Future from the Pull of the Past* (Harper Business, New York, 2011)

7 FROM TOUGH COMPETITION TO HYPERCOMPETITION

How to understand a fast-moving competitive landscape

In the face of the huge turbulence being encountered in many markets, Richard D'Aveni believed there are four axes of competition that should be considered.

These four axes are advantages based around price/quality, timing and know-how, strongholds and having deep pockets.

Let's start by considering the interaction between price and quality.

The following diagram shows a map of price versus value in order to position products within a market. The axes and the

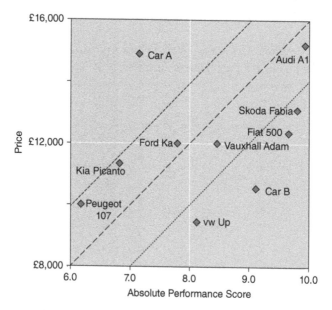

Figure 7.1 An example of a value map

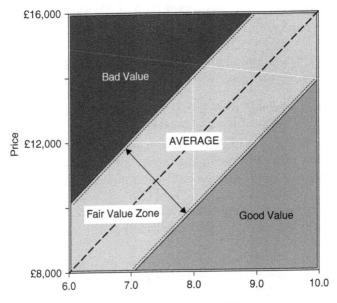

Figure 7.2 A value map illustrating the 'Fair Value' Zone

way of measuring the absolute performance will be specific for the market, but these are both applied consistently for different products. Diagram 7.1 positions some small cars with a view on performance against price. Don't get too fixated on the absolute positions – it's just an illustration in more ways than one.

The area of higher prices where performance drops is called the Bad Value Zone. Where performance is very high for the money, we get the Good Value Zone (as shown in 7.2).

So, back to D'Aveni's work and how cost and performance can interact in different ways.

Cost/quality

There are multiple ways in which the relationship can be played out by companies to try to find a unique positioning.

The first point to consider, and a bit of a classic marketing question, is whether the organization is a follower or a leader in the relationship between cost and quality. However, let's think about the relationship between these variables in other circumstances.

A price war will result in a vertical movement of a product or service down the map. Lower price for the same performance.

Different segments in terms of price and quality may exist – meaning you have some high-quality, high-price products and some low-cost and low-price ones. A variant of this would see a company producing multiple products with broadly similar ratios of price to quality – to essentially cover multiple niches.

An outflanking strategy could define products that lie outside the positions of current products in the market.

Over time, a product that remains static on the map will find it harder to compete as performance improves. The following diagram shows that shift. In reality, you would keep recalibrating the map to ensure the 'Fair Value Zone' represents a good approximation of the average product. A product that remains at the same price and quality would therefore migrate towards the top left in subsequent versions of the map, relative to newer competitors.

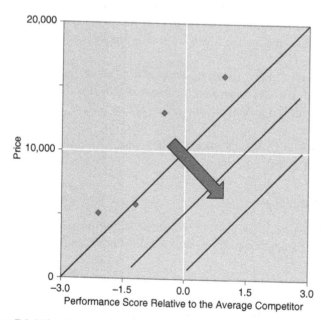

Figure 7.3 Value lines on a value map

Superior differentiation can occur where a company moves a product horizontally on the map – providing higher performance at the same (or similar) price. However, over time you could track the movement of competitors as value lines (see previous diagram) that track across the chart with each generation. Why do they move? Well you're assuming that each generation is delivering more than the previous ones and so you get this transition across the chart.

The problem with cost/quality plays

The challenge is safeguarding the erosion of differential advantages and the impact of price wars as products move towards being commodities. In the end, the ability to create a new benefit that actually matters to customers is eroded. There is just enough of whatever is required in the produce/service. For example, your tablet screen has a resolution of sufficient quality that you can't see any difference with a higher resolution screen.

When you get to this point, competition tends to occur along an 'ultimate' value line and moves to being mostly about price.

Timing and know-how

This relates to a number of aspects like **first-mover advantages**. If being first mover converts into early leadership then the secondary benefit could be superior economies of scale (if the organization has actively searched to exploit the economies). This could also involve the leader exploiting switching costs as early customers become locked into the company's products (e.g. buying the first of a next generation of video games system makes you unlikely to change).

However, time does move on and one generation of product may then be superseded by something better or be completely out-positioned by a superior technology, process, etc.

Strongholds

These represent areas that you can protect through barriers to entry – either natural or created by the company. That might be because a niche is too small for anyone else to consider exploiting.

Regional competition is typical of this approach, with competitors dominating their 'home' region. However, the natural drive for growth may cause one player to start engaging in another's market in an effort to increase revenues.

Deep pockets

This approach is based around mergers and acquisitions. Essentially, you are buying your way into a new position or are protecting an existing position. It also includes using your resources to dominate a market. That might be through price wars, or extreme spending on R&D, say (for example, Apple spending US$6 billion annually in this area).

If this approach were bulletproof in the long term, then we would not have seen major corporations disappear. Nokia was number 5 in the world for brand value in 2009. Then just a few years later, the dominant player in the smartphone market has left the building. Cash alone will only take you so far.

THINKING ABOUT INCREASINGLY COMPETITIVE ENVIRONMENTS
Another 7 S's

D'Aveni came up with his own 7 S's to consider ways of competing in these most challenging environments (not to be confused with McKinsey's 7-S model that is used to identify different aspects of the way a company operates and thinks). He quotes George Bernard Shaw: 'reasonable people adapt to the world, the unreasonable ones persist in trying to adapt the world to themselves'. In this regard, competition is going to require companies to become unreasonable.

The first two S's are for identifying advantage (without the assumption that it will be sustainable in the long term)

- Driving for superior Stakeholder satisfaction
- Strategic soothsaying

The direction is to find ways to deliver to unserved customers or new ways of serving existing ones. This search for new ways to deliver to existing ones is discussed elsewhere as the logical solution to the challenge when upstream aspects of business (economies of scale, dominant market power) can no longer guarantee success. The very question stops us concentrating too hard on the static aspects of how products are currently delivered and moves it forward.

The capability for disruption will be enhanced by building the following two attributes.

- **Positioning for Speed**
- **Positioning for Surprise**

The remainder of the 7 S's relate to how you act in a disruptive environment. This is about how you shape and manage the market as well as the actions of current and potential competitors.

- **Shifting the rules of the game**
- **Signalling the strategic intent**
- **Simultaneous and sequential strategic thrust**

However, the 7 S's also mean that you are trying to manage a set of contradictions and compromises.

Going faster means that you may make mistakes in terms of reducing quality for customers. You may change so quickly that you fail to take customers with you and perhaps disappoint stakeholders.

Soothsaying is that longer-term view, the ability to spend time looking into the future but a drive for speed or the strategic thrusts may mean you don't pay enough attention to the big things for the future.

If you are managing stakeholder satisfaction hard, this may lead to more rigid decision-making and checking that acts against swift decision-making. Similarly, this may limit your ability to surprise the market.

So what are the big takeaways here?

- **Change, change and change again.** Any company needs to keep re-inventing itself to remain relevant in markets where competitive advantages are eroded and imitation by competitors invalidates benefits.
- **Aligning an organization to respond to hypercompetivity will become very important.** The implicit compromises between different parts of the 7 S's mean that you are acting to identify how the 7 S's can best be tailored to your current setup and circumstances, in comparison to the competition. However, beyond this, the exceptional hypercompetitive company will seek to eliminate the need for trade-offs. This in itself provides a fascinating set of thinking behind a long-term strategic change within the organization to align itself for hypercompetitivity.
- **There will be more than 7 S's.** As with the Four P's of marketing (all 7 of them these days), and PEST analysis (which has inflated to include other factors beyond the original four), more S's are likely to be identified in the future. Even the model for dynamic competition is going to need to be dynamic!
- **Adopting the 7 S's approach will increase the symptoms of hypercompetition.** The ability to outperform competitors will be limited by how many adopt these approaches. The inescapable conclusion is that although not all companies will get the alignment of the 7 S's right, the fact that more and more are likely to try within a market will merely reinforce the other underlying drivers of turbulence.

Source

D'Aveni, Richard A., *Hyper-competition: Managing the Dynamics of Strategic Maneuvering* (The Free Press, New York, 1994)

See also

Chapter 8 – Discusses how to respond to a hypercompetitive environment.

Chapter 6 – Provides a background on disruptive forces in a market that further complicate the choice of strategy.

Further reading

D'Aveni, Richard A., *Beating the Commodity Trap: How to Maximize Your Competitive Position and Increase Your Pricing Power* (Harvard Business Review Press, Boston, 2010)

8 RESPONDING TO HYPERCOMPETITION

How turbulent markets mean cost focus is not the best option

This chapter will consider the effectiveness of cost-focused organizations compared to more innovative ones that are actively looking to change the market. It will also look at why companies' research into customer thinking has to change in order to match the realities of these turbulent times.

We've discussed the turbulent environment being faced in many organizations. This concept has been captured in a word that describes the more extreme versions of the phenomenon – hypercompetition. First coined by Richard D'Aveni in 1994, let's nail our understanding of what hypercompetition means.

D'Aveni's original premise suggested that the effects of globalization and deregulation help drive competition that can erode and overtake competitive advantage ever more quickly.

There is an interesting perspective of how hypercompetition impacts customer value from Kurt Matzler et al in 2009. They worked with 300 senior executives from Germanic countries in Western Europe to see how the execs were looking at the very dynamic environments around them. The execs surveyed came from a range of industries and also company sizes. The findings are interesting and relevant.

In 75 per cent of cases, the respondents suggested that the quality of what was being bought had been driven up in the previous three years but only 14.3 per cent within that 75 per cent said this had brought with it a corresponding increase in price. The interesting thing about the group that had raised quality and prices is that 56 per cent of them were performing above their respective industry average and 40 per cent were average. Only a few were poor performers.

This enabled the research team to identify the top performers ('innovators') and the rest ('optimizers').

What they discovered was that 80 per cent of the optimizers have a strong focus on process improvement and with that cost reduction. This mindset makes you focus on savings in the business but also, potentially, underinvestment in innovation. Most of the optimizers believed that further differentiation through product development or process improvement was impossible for them in their market.

What is worrying is that among the optimizers, just over a third had been able to reduce costs, 30 per cent had seen costs remain steady and a frustrated 26 per cent had actually seen costs go up. That cost increase had occurred even though 75 per cent of managers had implemented at least one cost-reduction programme.

THINKING ABOUT THE RIGHT APPROACH

There were a few sobering and occasionally depressing thoughts that emerged from the work.

The first thing is that the rush for cost savings as a dominating corporate principle is a weak approach. The correlation between sustained success and those that have downsized and/or outsourced is very limited.

The second thought is that the companies that did better were not simply looking to improve a process. Instead, they were aiming to find new processes. The authors quote economist Joseph Schumpeter's work and his emphasis on 'creative destruction'. As an example of this thinking, the CEO of Nokia did some creative destruction when announcing the company would no longer rely on its own Symbian software platform and would instead move to Windows. In change management projects, a metaphor used sometimes is that of a 'burning platform' – causing people to have to move whether they wish to or not. It's irrevocably gone so you have to be elsewhere.

In the case of Nokia and Symbian, the 'burning platform' actually was the abandonment of a platform.

A very interesting learning point was about the ability to do appropriate market research. To understand this fully we need first to relate some classic thinking from Everett Rogers.

His work in validating ideas about the diffusion of products has become widespread in business. This is in spite of the fact that the core thinking behind the diffusion curve is more than 50 years old. The curve shows the different stages of product diffusion – with products being taken up at first by innovators and then on a group-by-group basis until finally laggards are buying the product.

Now one thing to bear in mind is that the era of things like Twitter and Facebook means that this curve can be accelerated, stalled or stopped completely by the high-speed 'word of mouth' of the Internet age. Today, I suspect the exact percentages may therefore be different from those initially derived, particularly depending on the industry, the degree of trialability of the product, etc.

Each group along the diffusion curve has different characteristics. For example, the degree of risk aversion increases as you move from the innovators (fans of cutting-edge something or other) to the laggards (highly risk averse and wanting to see longer term reliability and acceptance of a product before they will buy it). In *Crossing the Chasm*, Geoffrey A. Moore refers to the 'Early Adopters' as visionaries and the 'Early Majority' as pragmatists. These descriptions rather nicely sum up the difference between the two.

Now back to Matzler et al again. The learning point from their work is that the diffusion curve will impact how you research products. If you ask a group to consider an innovative new product, the innovators are the natural audience for it. However the diffusion effect is about how long it takes the other groups to 'get' a product. So when faced with it for the first time, the majority of a focus group may simply say they don't like a product or be lukewarm about it. This is because only 2.5 per cent of any random group may have the innovator mindset (if we accept Rogers' figures for the sake of argument). The authors also point out that across a sample, some users with very specific requirements and/or strong preferences may be lost in the broad swathe of respondents.

So what? Well if you want to know about the next big thing, you don't talk to the laggards. The next big thing in their lives may be an electric toaster and they might finally be getting around to maybe connecting to the Internet. Okay, that's slightly facetious, but fundamentally correct. To think about big trends, you have to at least talk to the innovator group to see if it is susceptible to the offer. Does that mean you'll get the right answer? Actually, nope. Moore described the specific challenges of moving through the diffusion curve with high-tech products that are discontinuous innovations (ones that represent a significant shift, not just an evolution). He suggested that the transition from the 'Early Adopters' to 'Early Majority' is particularly difficult – likening it to a chasm that requires careful attention to cross successfully.

Many companies/technologies have not succeeded in the transition to the 'Early Majority'. For every product that crossed the chasm (like smartphones and digital video recorders such as TiVo), there will be many more failures such as Philips' LaserDiscs.

The thinking that comes from this type of learning was used by Audi when it used people from different parts of the diffusion curve to do different kinds of research for the company.

Innovators were used to provide thinking about the future of car infotainment systems. The next group, the early adopters were asked to comment on functionality for the systems such as voice activation, navigation, etc. That's the coming generation of product features, whereas the innovators were peeking over the horizon in terms of products. Heavy users were asked about the weaknesses of current systems. That's about the here and now.

So overall, the closer to the cutting edge of the innovators, the further into the future was the context of input for a particular group.

So what are the big takeaways here?

- **Cost savings and process improvement will only get you so far.** This is particularly true in a world where everyone is doing the same thing. You're chasing very marginal gains in some cases and the incremental improvement in each step may get smaller and smaller.
- **Winners are able to increase quality and price.** Okay that's a broad statement but the results are pretty clear in the findings. What doesn't work is sitting and imagining you can't do anything in your market. Markets do evolve towards being more commodity-like but you have to keep looking for ways to differentiate the company and/or products and services.

Sources

Gilbert, C., Eyring, M. & Foster R. N., 'Rebuild your core while you reinvent your business model', *Harvard Business Review*, December 2012

Matzler, K., Bailom, F., Anschober, M. & Richardson, S. 'Hypercompetition, customer-value competition, and the new role of market research', *Innovative Marketing*, Vol. 5 Issue 2 2009

Moore, Geoffrey A., *Crossing the Chasm: Marketing and Selling High-Tech Products to Mainstream Customers* (Harper Business, New York, 1998)

Wessel, M. & Christensen, Clayton M., 'Surviving Disruption', *Harvard Business Review*, December 2012

See also

Chapter 7 – Outlines the basic principles of hypercompetition.

Further reading

D'Aveni, Richard A., *Beating the Commodity Trap: How to Maximize Your Competitive Position and Increase Your Pricing Power* (Harvard Business Review Press, Boston, 2010)

D'Aveni, Richard A., *Hyper-competition: Managing the Dynamics of Strategic Maneuvering* (The Free Press, New York, 1994)

9 EXPLOITING DISRUPTION

Don't suffer from disruption in your industry – exploit it!

Companies can sit and let disruption affect them or they can find ways to fight back. Waiting passively for bad things to happen to you is clearly not a great approach.

Chapter 12 will look at Michael Porter's view that a company should stick to one of three generic strategies for delivering competitive advantage. These are competing through cost leadership, seeking differentiation or exploiting niches. A very clear signal from his work is the danger of attempting to be all things to all men. Trying to do all three is a dangerous position and Porter strongly advocates just following one approach.

So Porter's main lesson from that work would suggest that the twin-track approach to coping with disruption (and that advocated in Chapter 12) is wrong.

Just as it seems we're about to square up for a serious disagreement, Porter actually recognizes that you can have different business units that operate and compete in fundamentally different ways.

There is a weight of research that supports the twin-track approach. For example, Clayton Christensen calls this approach the innovator's solution in the face of the challenge of disruption ('the innovator's dilemma').

But just when we can assume that this is the correct approach for all, there is work to provide some caution about the applicability and effectiveness of separating business models into a twin-track approach.

Markides and Oyon questioned whether all responses to disruption that follow the twin-track approach work and whether you can respond without the creation of a new 'disruptive' business unit. Their findings are slightly sobering and provide a good sanity check in what might otherwise be a headlong rush to separation.

They discuss the airline industry where, for example, established national carriers have tried to respond to the rise of low-cost airlines by creating their own version. For example, British Airways tried this with its low-cost operator Go and KLM followed a similar approach with Buzz. These are separated businesses where the disruptive part essentially failed.

The Accor hotel group illustrates the ability to combine multiple brands across the whole range from luxury with Sofitel down to utility with F1 (that's cheap and cheerful) without separation.

The work suggests that companies that succeed with the twin-track approach are likely to give more financial and operational independence to the different business units than those that do not succeed.

In fact their findings could be summarized as achieving higher levels of real autonomy while taking opportunities for that most elusive commodity – synergies!

However, they also suggest that common rewards and incentives programmes across the two business units should be applied. This goes against the view that the two should compete aggressively. A concern must be that the new business unit's actions are somehow watered down by having to 'play nicely' with the core business. However, a bigger problem is about setting appropriate yet common metrics across two different business units. The influence of metrics on how people act and the potential for unintended consequences cannot be overstated.

For example, the drive to share resources may mean that both business units are measured on use of a common resource. This happens in the media world where an in-house design team may exist within a larger group of companies. Efficiency wise it makes sense to force everyone to use this resource but the result appears to be inefficiency. The design function has no real need to compete so can charge these 'internal' clients whatever it likes, be less responsive and potentially worse than an outside design house hungry for the same business.

The logic of the cost savings leads to the wrong result!

DON'T AUTOMATICALLY DIVE INTO A DISRUPTED MARKET

The findings provide us with some questions that can be used to assess potential moves for a 'traditional' company faced with the reality of a disruptive business model.

1. Should a company enter a segment served by the disruptive business model?

_____

_____

_____

_____

_____

_____

This considers the fundamental point that the new market may not be attractive for an existing business. This unattractiveness may be because of the scope of the market, the revenues and margins possible from exploiting it or characteristics of the customers. For example, once customers start using any kind of online price aggregator, their loyalty may shift to that site rather than to the services they purchase from it. It may therefore be difficult for one provider to capture price sensitive customers and to retain them, given they will do a search across the market when it comes to renew any contract/subscription.

Another challenge is to consider how well the company can deliver into the new market. You may have no ability to compete effectively. The new market may be radically different in terms of client type, needs and preferences. Rather than an evolution of the current market (that a company may understand very well), the new space may be revolutionary and very far removed from the company's capabilities.

2. Should the company attack the new market with a new business model or will the traditional one work?

_____

_____

_____

_____

_____

This is a trickier question. In the airline industry, union rules, working practices, processes, salaries and fare structures are very different between the traditional national carriers and the newer low-cost operators. The former were generally built on monopolies in protected routes, and even since these have been opened up are about a more premium experience, and hence price. The low-cost competitors try to maximize Passenger Seat Kilometres (PSK) that represent a paying passenger in a seat in the air. That means a focus on efficiency of turnaround to sweat the main assets (the planes) as hard as possible. The ethos and approach of these two types of carrier is so different that national carriers have often chosen to create a whole new business unit rather than deliver to two such different categories within one traditional organization.

3. Should the company copy the disruptive business model to exploit the new market?

_____

_____

_____

_____

_____

The concern here should be that you are creating a 'me too' business that has no strong points of differentiation to the disrupter.

Actually, there is a great opportunity to look at the strengths and weaknesses of the disrupter's approach to the market and do it better. Just because they have created the new market doesn't necessarily mean they have got it right.

4. How far removed should the new business model be from the traditional one?

_____

_____

_____

_____

_____

_____

This is the core issue about the sharing of resources discussed in Chapter 10.

The suggestion is that you maximize the sharing of resources that allows both the traditional and disruptive business model to work effectively while managing key resources. The challenge is the creeping erosion of independence of a new business if you take individual steps that all seem logical in trying to avoid reinventing the wheel. It's very easy to go too far and end up completely replicating the traditional business, but sensible sharing, in particular of scarce resources, should be pursued without compromising the independence of the new business unit.

5. If a new business unit is created, what challenges will arise in following two different business models at the same time?

_____

_____

_____

_____

_____

_____

_____

_____

_____

_____

When you've answered these questions, you'll be some way along the road to knowing whether you should enter the market and how to do it. The pros and cons of your choices should be clearer.

So what are the big takeaways here?

- **Structure your response.** Use the questions above as a framework when considering how to respond to a disruptive business model threatening your core business.
- **Think about how you might screw up this approach.** It seems a glib question but if you ask people this seriously, they will think about the traditional weaknesses of the company that may hamper development of the new business. That might be cultural, processes, metrics, personal attributes, skills or whatever… but you absolutely want to understand why exploiting this disruption might be hard for you. Following a similar logic, ask how you are likely to succeed – to capture thinking about how the disruption might be a good fit.
- **Don't do the same… do better!** Think about whether the disrupter has achieved the most disruptive position or if there is a 'better' positioning that could be achieved if you entered the market. This question tries to stop companies just doing a 'me too' business in response to a disrupter. Sometimes you can do better and you should approach this challenge not just to match but to better a disrupter if you can.

Sources

Christensen, Clayton M., *The Innovator's Dilemma: When New Technologies Cause Great Firms to Fail* (Harvard Business Review Press, Boston, 1997)

Downes, L. & Nunes, Paul F., 'Big-Bang Disruption – A new kind of innovator can wipe out incumbents in a flash', *Harvard Business Review*, March 2013

Markides, C. C. & Oyon, D. (Summer 2010), 'What to Do Against Disruptive Business Models (When and How to Play Two Games at Once)' *MIT Sloane Management Review*

See also

Chapter 7 – Take a look to understand more about what disruption means

Chapter 8 – And how to survive it

Further reading

Christensen, Clayton & Raynor, Michael E., *The innovator's solution: creating and sustaining successful growth* (Harvard Business School Press, Boston, 2003)

10 ROUTES TO RESILIENCE

How to hedge your bets successfully when everything is at stake

As discussed in Chapter 5, success can be very dangerous as it can blind you to the need to change. It's also more difficult to convince people to take tough choices when things are apparently good. What is certain is that almost every company will need to undergo serious change at some point and the ability to time this right and execute it correctly will have a major impact on the longer-term survival of the business.

The potential for disruption is one possible trigger for such changes. The last couple of chapters have discussed the impact of disruption and also some techniques for identifying how to understand and potentially counteract it.

In work by Gilbert, Eyring and Foster, they suggest a third way they believe is a more 'resilient' approach, where it is not a choice between a legacy and a new business approach. In their thinking, both are pursued but in an intelligent way. Before looking at some of the subtleties they suggest, consider the problems you would face in trying to implement this type of twin-track.

Let's think practically about businesses and their capacity to change. In most cases, businesses have been down-sized, right-sized, made lean, optimized or whatever management term you wish to use. Very few have spare resources or any 'fat' in the organization. Now this makes sense in financial terms but imagine you are trying to change the company. Everyone is likely to be very busy doing their thing in the organization and changing the direction can be akin to redirecting a supertanker. Even relatively simple change will take a while and deeper changes can take years to propagate completely. You don't have the right resources. You don't have the spare time. You don't have the experience.

The culture and 'that's how we do things around here' approach to doing things should not be underestimated as any major transformation is going to need to overcome this. However, there is also the legacy business to consider. Do you abandon it by focusing on the new thing? Will it wither away more quickly if you take attention from it?

Let's consider two distinct cases to start.

The first is where the company cannot or simply does not change direction in time and hits the rocks. This is obviously the wrong result, but if you look at Kodak you could argue that it was killed by not embracing the change to digital photography. The irony of this is that Kodak invented the technology but held on too stubbornly to the traditional photography market as it was hugely profitable for them. In Chapter 5 we discuss the challenge of trying to change a business when it's doing well but even if this is not the case, many companies have simply failed to change in time.

The second scenario is where the whole company shifts direction and emphasis to try to exploit the new situation. In this case, the struggles with the adjustments and challenges of that shift are exacerbated by the 'abandonment' of the legacy business and potentially the limited revenues available from the new area in its early stages. This approach requires deep pockets and strong stomachs. This may seem daunting but it is the level of major change required by some businesses to confront the shifting markets and customer preferences in front of them.

If you fail to configure the 'new' business area correctly you risk repeating the failings of the legacy business or not competing as effectively as new entrants into the market. In spite of good intentions, configuring a new business can often become cutting and pasting structures and processes from the old business onto the new one, copying over all the problems and limitations at the same time.

A second concern is where the two entities are competing for customers and resources. If you have two businesses measured on financial results that are chasing the same customer in different ways, then you risk them damaging one another as badly as if they were bitter competitors.

Gilbert, Eyring and Foster's approach is to aim for a parallel approach that combines the best of both worlds.

The first piece part of their approach looks at transforming the core business to match the new market situation it is facing. This is not something that may be easy or quick to achieve but is preferable to abandoning the current business area (and associated revenues) completely. The authors refer to this as 'Transformation A'.

The second leg of this strategy is unsurprisingly called 'Transformation B'. This is about creating a new, standalone business unit that is designed to fully exploit the disruption.

So far, this just looks like trying to ride two horses at the same time. However, remember that many companies have been disrupted by a new entrant with no competitive response from them and so the act of creating a new business, even if it might cannibalize the revenues of the core business, is already a far-sighted approach in comparison.

Where the subtlety comes in is in the use of resources. The creation of a new, standalone business unit can often be undermined bit by bit as the idea of cost-sharing leads to decisions to share costs, people, offices, etc. and before you know it you've replicated the old organization (and all its faults) in the new organization. However, trying to create a completely independent business unit may be difficult where resources can be shared effectively or where these are scarce. In the latter case, the risk is that there is immediate conflict and a clear sense that, say, the core business wins and the new unit loses (or vice versa).

Gilbert et al recognized this problem and suggested the formation of a 'Capabilities Exchange'. This means both the core and the new unit can draw on scarce resources that are designated as common to both. This is clearly better than a situation where the core or new operation has to continually negotiate with the other part for access to these resources.

The strength of this twin-track approach is clear.

- The core business continues to generate revenues while the new operation is being established.
- Each part is able to develop its own strategy independently.
- In the event that the new operation fails, the overall business is insulated as it still has the core business generating revenues.

The research includes discussion of US firm Barnes & Noble (B&N). It was a traditional book retailer that still maintains some 675 retail stores across the US and 686 outlets in universities and colleges[1].

The classic challenge of selling through retail stores in the online era has been multiplied with the rise of the ebook market, driven by Amazon's Kindle as well as by smartphones and tablets that can also be used as ereaders. In the face of this, Barnes & Noble could have simply stuck to its existing strategy (as perhaps Borders did to its cost) but instead it responded to this 'perfect storm' of disruption by launching its own ereader (the Nook) and aimed to compete with Amazon on ebook sales.

Microsoft invested US$300 million into B&N but has not proceeded with any special devices. Samsung announced a deal with the company in 2014 and the thought is this gives B&N the chance to compete with Amazon's Kindle tablets with a branded product – but without the need to pay development costs.

What this move means for the company in the long term is open to question. Quarterly profit year on year for the retail business was down from US$181 million to US$168 million by January 25 2014. At the same time, the NOOK digital business reduced losses from US$200 to US$72 million[2]. Meanwhile, Microsoft dissolved the partnership with Barnes & Noble[3].}

HOW TO JUGGLE PRIORITIES AND RESOURCES

At the heart of Gilbert et al's approach is the effective setup and running of the Capabilities Exchange. The success or otherwise of this is likely to heavily influence the outcomes for the core and new operations. They suggested a five-step process.

The right leadership

The exchange is likely to be a contentious and challenging area and so requires very senior leadership to arbitrate disputes and disagreements. This is probably going to be the CEO as those at the next level down may lack the positional power and/or perceived authority to manage the situation. In addition to the CEO of the overall business, the person heading up the disruptive business and the person leading the transformation of the core business should be on the leadership team.

Identifying resources

The second and logical step is to identify the resources that both operations will need and that can be shared. The particular focus here is not to just think about IT or HR or things like that. Yes, sharing those will potentially save some operating expenditure for the new entity, but few businesses achieve epic success by embarking on cost-saving programmes. This twin-track approach is about a bold strategic move and so the key resources are those that can help the disruptive business outperform its competition.

As an example of a key resource, Gilbert cites Barnes & Noble's floor space in its stores. It is able to use these retail outlets as a means for customers to hold the Nook ereader and experience the screen quality, ease of use and lightness. This means they have to forego display space for traditional books and so you can see the natural tension between the two competing uses. However, Barnes & Noble has decided the improved likelihood of converting a customer to its Nook through being able to experience the product outweighs any associated loss of traditional book sales.

Team creation

The third step is to create teams to manage the exchange and the allocation of specific resources. These should consist of people from both the core and disruptive business to ensure there is a balance of interests and hence actions. The teams themselves are like project teams in that they are created flexibly and continue to exist while there is a need for them. When the need is gone, say because a resource is no longer needed by one or other party, the team should be gone too.

Establish boundaries

The fourth step is to protect the boundaries of the two parties. You want both to operate and compete as if the overall company's future depends on them. That's maybe not far from the truth but the problem with such aggressive competition is that it needs to be managed effectively. As mentioned previously, the only person with the positional power sufficient to separate a warring core and disruptive businesses is likely to be the CEO.

If you don't have a true spirit of each business being critical, you end up with a situation like Kodak, where a potentially disruptive part of the business (digital) is insufficiently supported, leaving the core of film and paper sales to wither over time. Kodak tried to pick just one horse to ride and switched too late and in too half-hearted a way to catch up for the poor decision they made earlier.

The winner

The final step is to recognize that the future is likely to lie with the disruptive business. Although the core business may remain profitable for longer due to the transformation activities, the disruptive business area has been identified as capable of changing the fundamentals in the sector in some way. Improving the core business is still only a stop gap if the disruptive business really starts to succeed.

So what are the big takeaways here?

- **Siblings will fight and so will competing companies in the same group.** If you don't have a mechanism to minimize these disagreements then you're going to have one or other party permanently sitting on the 'naughty step'.
- **Only the 500-pound gorilla can keep the peace.** The CEO of the overall group is the only person that can control and direct the two competing business units.

Sources

Gilbert, C., Eyring, M. & Foster R. N., 'Rebuild your core while you reinvent your business model', *Harvard Business Review*, December 2012

Wessel, M. and Christensen, Clayton M., 'Surviving Disruption', *Harvard Business Review*, December 2012

Barnes & Noble stats:

[1] www.reuters.com/finance/stocks/overview?symbol=BKS.N

[2] Barnes and Noble Annual Report (10Q) for the Period Ending 01/25/14

[3] http://www.cnet.com/uk/news/microsoft-barnes-noble-end-nook-marriage-for-62-million/

See also

Chapter 6 – Describes the phenomenon of disruption in detail

Chapter 9 – Discusses some ways that it can be used to your advantage

Further reading

Christensen, Clayton M., *The Innovator's Dilemma: When New Technologies Cause Great Firms to Fail* (Harvard Business Review Press, Boston, 1997)

11 SEEING DISRUPTION COMING

Why classic strategy doesn't make your business bulletproof

In the early chapters of the book, we discuss the simple dangers of companies that fail to really plan strategically.

The process of considering changes in your immediate business environment and responding to them should not resemble rocket science (and it isn't – even if it is often badly done). However, a more difficult challenge is to identify potential sources of disruption in a market before someone else does. These are not simple evolutions but are seismic shifts in how business can be done.

Being able to identify these gives you the chance to take advantage or prepare to respond before it's too late. Failing to do so is not so clever.

Clayton Christensen has suggested a framework that builds on his work on disruption in *The Innovator's Dilemma*. It measures a company against the disruptive opportunity – recognizing that some disruptions may fatally hit a company head on, whereas others may be more minor impacts or even a near miss.

To predict what will happen with a particular disruption, Christensen suggests the following:

- define the disruptive business model and its strengths
- compare these strengths to your own competitive advantages (as genuinely perceived by customers rather than believed by people inside the company)
- Identify the circumstances that would make it easier or harder for a disruptive company to overtake your current competitive advantages or create new ones.

Marketing theory talks about the fundamental or 'core' benefits of a product or service and Christensen uses this to define the concept of an 'extendable core' for a disrupter. This phrase describes the parts of the business model that can help a disrupter continue to compete effectively as it expands into new parts of the market over time. In other words, the core benefit in the original niche is also applicable and valued in new ones the disrupter migrates into.

If the fundamental advantages of the disrupter's approach are widely applicable, they will be able to dominate as it expands across new segments. However, in the absence of an extendable core, the disrupter will not be able to leave the initial niche it has found and so the danger to 'traditional' competitors will be limited.

In simple terms, defining how extendable the core is will tell you which customers the disrupter is liable to capture and also those it will not be able to attract.

Identifying the true needs of customers and serving them in a new way is at the heart of marketing and indeed is vital for disruption. However, as Henry Ford said, if he'd have asked people what they wanted, they would have said a faster horse (rather than a nice black Model T). Disruption can shift the key need in a market and so companies should not just focus on the current priorities of customers. They should think about the fundamental need being met and then innovate around new ways to deliver against this.

The good news is that you can put in place the processes and approaches necessary to find the disruption that will help you survive and thrive within fast-growing markets – or that might enable a new entrant to take your market. Chapter 5 discusses why market leaders may fail to respond to these but let's talk about how to identify these opportunities, on the assumption companies will be smart enough to respond to them in the right way.

IDENTIFYING THE DISRUPTIONS ON THE HORIZON

If spotting potential disruptions early, and responding to them correctly sounds hard, then let me reinforce the fact that it is! Many businesses have failed to spot the 'next big thing' in their industry. But what would be stupid is if they weren't even looking in the first place. There's no excuse, you have to look out and keep looking.

You need sophisticated thinking across a number of different parts of the existing business landscape to predict the disruptive opportunity, understand the timing of it and the impact it is likely to have.

We need an approach to predict the scale and effect of a disruption that then inputs into the overall strategy process.

At a simple level, if you look at your company's participation in each of the segments that would be under threat from the disrupter, you can identify the revenue, market share, volume, profit margin, etc. that is at risk in each.

Now the extendable core cannot be considered in isolation as it will also depend on the nature and strengths of your own competitive advantage within each additional segment that could be entered.

In addressing the question about the durability of your competitive advantage in the face of a disruptive competitive threat, you can address the following questions about whether there are any barriers to the disruption (and how strong these are):

- Is there a momentum barrier (where customers are very used to, and comfortable with, how things are done at present)?
- Is there a technical development or implementation barrier?
- Is there an ecosystem barrier (see discussion of Airbnb's ecosystem below)?

- Is there a new technology barrier (meaning the technology needed to underpin a disruption does not currently exist)?
- Is there a business model barrier? Are the economies of scale, reach or other aspects of your business difficult to replicate for the disrupter?

To understand how you can apply this thinking, let's look about these barriers with the example of how Airbnb was able to grow to a higher market capitalization (around US$10 billion in late 2014) than Marriott Group without having a single hotel room.

The hotels market was previously understood as being stratified into different price points, roughly corresponding to a star rating for different comfort, quality and amenity levels. Some hotel chains have a number of different brands that target these different price levels (e.g. Accor group goes from luxury with Sofitel through descending levels of luxury via Pullman, Novotel and Ibis down to the bargain F1 chain).

Creating a direct competitor or modifying the position of an individual hotel or brand will have its challenges and the market was relatively stable with a known capacity of rooms available to cater for business and leisure travellers in a location.

The disruption that was missed by many was Airbnb's fast growth from a 'couchsurfer' service through to connector of travellers to people letting out rooms, apartments or even complete homes. This created a sudden huge potential number of competitors. An article in June 2014 in the *San Francisco Chronicle*[1] analysed Airbnb's own data and identified 5,000 rentals on offer with two-thirds of these being complete apartments or houses. Compare this to around 33,000 hotel rooms reported in the city limits in late 2012[2].

So let's look at Airbnb's disruption against the five types of barrier described previously.

Momentum barrier

There is clearly an issue in 'trusting' that you will get a quality experience in someone else's home as they are not professional hosts. However, with 94 per cent of us believing in peer reviews (compared to just 14 per cent trusting advertising)[3], Airbnb has built up reviews to help overcome this trust issue. In the other direction, early bad publicity for 'renters' suffering damage to properties was mitigated with the introduction of a £600,000 insurance policy (or 'Hosts Guarantee' as the company terms it)[4].

Technical development or implementation barrier

Creation of large, content-rich websites is understood and relatively mature and so there is no particular technical barrier. For example, sites like eBay have demonstrated how to manage payments between buyers and sellers. In theory, laws should be preventing some renters from providing their properties as this contravenes the terms of their lease. In practice, many renters have ignored this constraint and the problem has created significant controversy in cities that are trying to manage the legal aspect aggressively. For example, Airbnb is illegal in Berlin but legal in San Francisco as I write this.

Ecosystem barrier

Airbnb is such a strong brand and website that it does not matter that the company is not present on travel aggregator websites (such as Hotels.com) or even aggregator of aggregator sites (trivago.com). Failure to be on these sites would be a disadvantage for a hotel but Airbnb does not need to be part of these providers' sites. There is no serious ecosystem barrier for Airbnb but any potential competitor may find it harder to replicate its model as it now dominates the sector it created.

Technology barrier

There isn't a technology barrier. What needs to exist to support Airbnb's approach is already in place. We have wide access to devices that connect us to the Internet and enable us to browse and book almost anywhere at any time.

Business model barrier

The business model appears to be a barrier when you think about competing in the accommodation market in the traditional way. In that model, you have to build hotels and populate them at high occupancy rates while delivering a consistent experience at the right price. However, Airbnb is truly disruptive and needs aggressive consideration of alternative ways of satisfying users' needs – rather than consideration of 'me too' businesses.

So what are the big takeaways here?

- **Look beyond 'business as usual'.** Put in place processes and a group tasked to assess potential disruptions to the organization's products/services.
- **Figure out how bad it might be.** When identified, potential disruptions should be fully described and quantified to understand the level of threat/opportunity they might represent.
- **Look beyond the current reality.** I find using 'what ifs' useful in these cases. Assume your business can be disrupted and ask questions such as, 'if costs in our market had fallen by 50 per cent in a year's time, how would that have happened?' or 'if we had been put out of business in three years, what would have killed us?'. The interesting thing is that answers that are off the topic of disruption may still be interesting and relevant.
- **Barriers that exist today may be eliminated tomorrow.** Things change. For example, costs may reduce down to the point that an approach becomes economic or another business model may affect yours. Google has been able to provide traffic data to drivers by picking up GPS data from people in cars using Google Maps for navigation. It's a 'free' side-benefit of the map application to them but has a big impact on competitors TomTom and Garmin.

Sources

Gilbert, C., Eyring, M. & Foster R. N., 'Rebuild your core while you reinvent your business model', *Harvard Business Review* , December 2012

Wessel, M. & Christensen, C. M., 'Surviving Disruption', *Harvard Business Review*, December 2012

[1] www.sfchronicle.com/business/item/airbnb-san-francisco-30110.php

[2] www.sanfrancisco.travel/research

[3] www.socialnomics.net

[4] https://www.airbnb.co.uk/guarantee

See also

Chapter 1 – Talks about the syndrome of 'rolling budgets'

Chapter 2 – Touches on companies that seem to think a strapline is an effective replacement for a properly thought through strategy and strategy process. The lack of the latter is particularly dangerous as the situation will change for all organizations and even if your strategy is appropriate today, it is unlikely to perfectly fit market conditions in even a year's time. These chapters show why companies can do so badly at selecting the right strategy.

Chapter 10 – Looks at how companies can exploit opportunities created by disruption using a twin-track response, as well as how to make sure this works well. This approach involves looking to transform the core business while also investing in the creation of a new 'disruptive' business unit.

Further reading

Christensen, Clayton M., *The Innovator's Dilemma: When New Technologies Cause Great Firms to Fail* (Harvard Business School Press, Boston, 1997)

12 PICKING WHICH COMPETITIVE ADVANTAGE TO PURSUE

You can't be good at everything – and you shouldn't try

A now classic but still very influential approach to considering the implications of different strategic choices was created by Michael E. Porter, a professor at Harvard University, in his book *Competitive Advantage*. This book probably packs in more important business models than any other and I'd suggest is a 'must read', alongside his book *Competitive Strategy*.

Porter put forward some generic approaches to serving a market and outlined some of the respective pros and cons of each approach. He believes creation of specific competitive advantages is a vital step in moving from a broad strategic direction into an effective plan of action. He's correct. What is clear since the book was written is that it can be increasingly difficult in some industries to find a position that provides that competitive advantage – one that can be maintained. We'll look at that in more detail in Chapter 14. For now, let's look at the three broad mechanisms for creating advantage.

Differentiation

This is a market-based approach that creates:

- one or more aspects of the product/service that is perceived as unique or of higher value than competitive offerings
- reasons for customers to choose the product instead of a competitive offering.

Cost leadership

Here the company aims to achieve:

- the lowest costs for production and distribution
- economies of scale (actively managing the supply chain to drive prices down as volumes increase)
- cost minimization across the company.

Focus

The level of focus refers to the breadth of the market that the organization will address. This may be from a narrowly defined niche through to mass market coverage. Within the scope defined, the organization can then deliver to the market via either of the two strategies described above – differentiation or cost leadership.

A focus strategy is therefore actually one of two variations – cost focus and differentiation focus.

The key learning point was that Porter stressed the importance of not attempting to follow all strategies at the same time. The demands on the organization for each are very different. However, he suggested that companies that fail to aggressively follow any of the three generic approaches would be 'stuck in the middle' and might struggle to compete effectively. A nuanced point is that in larger organizations different strategies might be relevant to different business units. But within each one, Porter's view is likely to be fundamental.

THINKING ABOUT THE 'CLASSIC' STRATEGIC CHOICES

Although following one of the strategies appears to be sensible, they are still not without their own risks.

Strategies	Potential risks associated with following the strategy
Differentiation	Competitors imitate the differentiation.
	Differentiating factors become less important for current buyers or new buying groups are less impressed by the company's offerings.
	Costs increase to deliver the differentiation – reaching a point where buyers do not value the differentiation enough to buy the product once it becomes more expensive.
Cost Leadership	Cost advantages are eroded by competitors – you lose your edge. Technological change – leading to the product being out-flanked suddenly. High competitor differentiation – meaning cost is not the most important criteria for potential buyers.
	Spending on R&D too low – leading to an inability to maintain differentiation.
Focus	Segments may become less attractive over time as the market changes and competitive strategies take effect. Competitors may re-segment or sub-segment the market. For example, consider the traditional market for large estate cars that was dominated by Volvo and Mercedes. It has recently been sliced into numerous sub-segments, including people carriers of all sizes (e.g. SUVs and 4 X4s). Competitors may imitate.

The different generic approaches outlined previously are all simple enough to understand but are more difficult to actually achieve. Let's look at some of the complexities in pursuing these strategies.

Aiming for cost reductions

Cost reductions do not happen automatically and so companies need to actively focus attention on one or more of the following areas:

1. Improving production efficiency – e.g. making larger quantities may enable a company to move from batch production (making a number at a time) through to something closer to a full production line.
2. Economies of scale – buying in greater quantities should allow a company to gain better discounts from suppliers.

The suppliers can improve their own production efficiency, allowing them to pass on cost reductions if they are themselves making larger orders.

3. Increasing the utilization of resources – for example, low-cost airlines aim to increase the time their aircraft are in the air. Legal firms will seek to increase the billable hours for their lawyers.

4. Advantages based on relationships to other Strategic Business Units (SBUs) – such as production expertise, better quality materials, advance notice of changes, etc.

5. First-mover advantages – the first mover can sometimes gain exclusive access to a technology or other part of the value chain (e.g. sign up the number one supermarket in the country to act as a distributor). However, you need to be careful as history is littered with companies that have tried the 'leading edge' of a technology and discovered it is more of a 'bleeding edge'. This failure to perform may be because the technology and associated processes are not mature enough for production or the market does not take to the new technology.

6. Physical location – this may be to do with distribution costs (so being close to a major transport hub would be beneficial) or being close enough to customers to provide them with rapid after-sales support.

Diseconomies of scale

Diseconomies of scale are the logical reversal of economies of scale. Beyond a certain point, growing bigger can actually hamper the effort to deliver.

For example, small companies don't tend to be weighed down with complex IT and HR policies and don't need to have carefully defined processes for doing everything. The number of employees is low enough that everyone probably understands what needs to be done and roughly who does what. However, as you add people to a task, you find that the need to coordinate the efforts will start to become more and more significant.

So what are the big takeaways here?

- **You can't be all things to all men.** Recognize that a position where you try to follow all three generic strategies will compromise your ability to compete. Identify which approach you are trying to follow and check to see if you are trying to 'ride two horses at the same time' – are you pursuing different generic strategies at the same time?
- **Don't take a static position.** You need to actively pursue improvements in your position or you risk being caught and even overtaken. Ask yourself whether you have projects and programmes in place to further enhance or at least maintain your competitive advantage? Is this source of advantage under threat?
- **Prioritize what you pursue hard but don't neglect any part of the business.** Just because you are pursuing one primary source of competitive advantage does not mean you forget the other two dimensions. For example, a company following a differentiation focus strategy should not ignore any efforts for cost reduction. They absolutely should. Subtly, the cost reduction in that case is not the primary way the business will compete, and so should be considered in the context of delivering the sources of differentiation. The business should accrue cost savings aggressively but only up to the point that further savings would erode or affect the differentiation.

Source

Porter, Michael E., *Competitive Advantage* (The Free Press, Cambridge, 1985)

See also

Chapter 21 – This discusses a variant of Porter's thinking. It's an interesting approach to thinking about where your business should focus and the projects and programmes it should be running as a result.

Chapter 22 – Provides an interesting perspective on how strategic thinking has moved on from classic concepts that work well in relatively static environments. It outlines some of the challenges and limitations of these approaches in more dynamic market conditions.

Chapter 6 – Describes the concept of disruption that is one of the mechanisms that is driving these more dynamic market situations.

Further reading

Christensen, Clayton M., *The Innovator's Dilemma: When New Technologies Cause Great Firms to Fail* (Harvard Business Review Press, Boston, 1997)

Porter, Michael E., *Competitive Strategy: Techniques for Analyzing Industries and Competitors* (The Free Press, New York, 2004)

13 WHAT IS THE THEORY OF YOUR FIRM?

'There is nothing so practical as a good theory'
Kurt Lewin

Growth is not always a good thing. Todd Zenger, a professor at Washington University, has looked at the concept of growth and considered how an overriding focus on it can set a company off in the wrong direction.

Now a search for growth is not a complete surprise or stupid since senior teams are all for 'maximizing shareholder value'. That's code for making the share price go up. That's code for making the shareholders rich. That's code for keeping your job.

Stable revenues mean stable share prices. New things, growth, potential for growth... they fuel an increase in share price and the key stakeholders will therefore be happy (we assume).

Zenger quotes Michael Porter's concern that searching for growth can blunt a company's focus, causing it to look at markets that are less attractive or serve customers who don't value their product or services as much as their current customers. So you may move to markets that are less and less attractive just to find that elusive extra revenue.

Zenger points out that Porter, although correct, doesn't actually address the conundrum he describes. Zenger's view is slightly at odds with some of the other ideas in the book in that he doesn't focus on the search for new ways to create value for the business.

He calls his ideas the 'corporate theory' – helping steer an organization to select strategies. The better the theory, the better the selection, the better the organization will perform. Nothing too rocket science so far, but let's dig into the research.

Zenger talks about companies that get into trouble as they lose track of the theory of value creation that brought them initial success. He believes that turnaround operations often focus on reverting to that original 'corporate theory'.

His view is that the corporate theory covers how managers create value by making the best use of a finite set of resources and capabilities.

Now a good theory will encapsulate two things – foresight and insight.

Foresight means you have a view about what will be happening in the particular segment or industry. This entails being able to formulate a picture of how the industry will evolve over time and the impact this will have on the underlying drivers of business success. What will happen to customer numbers? How will the needs as well as the capabilities of products/services change? How will customer requirements alter?

It should consider the future roadmap for current and potential future technologies relevant to the industry and what the probable responses of your competitors might be. The latter point is critical but I'm always surprised by how many companies come up with a cunning plan and assume nobody will copy it.

The UK supermarket scene in early 2015 is a bloodbath of lost margins as pretty much all the players are now price-matching to the others. That means everybody's margins are eroded but, as everyone is doing the same thing, there is no differential advantage. Someone's bright idea to win market share using this approach hasn't really created any shifts in share among the major players. Instead it has tanked their margins and not addressed the real problem for them – the rise of relatively new players like Aldi and Lidl.

Insight involves figuring out which of the company's rare/unique resources can be used to optimize the company's position in that future.

The reason this is more specific than simply resources, is that those that are common across the company and its competitors will not easily give rise to a value-creating position. Why is that? Well they can simply copy what you do. So insight should be more subtle in considering the edge your organization has in terms of resources – the distinct pieces you can move in this huge chess game.

Cross-sight (an odd phrase I admit, just go with it) is then the next stage – using the company's assets to create value or acquiring new ones that complement the existing ones.

DEVELOPING A CORPORATE THEORY

So what might a 'corporate theory' look like? Let's apply this thinking to a case Zenger discussed in his work where he talked about Apple. I'm not sure many companies have inspired more words that try to capture the company's approach – and most of which fail. Now it's not that I know the 'right' answer. I think it's that the company is unique and has captured so many interesting aspects of brand, positioning, design and technology that it seems quite hard to explain in a simple way.

In spite of this, Zenger's elegant corporate theory for Apple makes a lot more sense than most views on the iconic firm.

He believes that Steve Jobs's corporate theory was that: 'Consumers would pay a premium for ease of use, reliability, and elegance in computing and other digital devices and the best means for delivering these was relatively closed systems, significant vertical integration and tight control over design.'

Re-read that. That's a pretty good theory that constrains the actions of the company while considering both where markets would go, and the all-important 'how' Apple would go about it.

The foresight on how customer needs would change was combined with a view that computers would become consumer goods. However, this was combined with a view that something that was well designed would be very attractive to consumers. The key insight was to recognize the potential for design to contribute to value creation. However, this also bled over into thinking about how the software should be similarly elegant and so Jobs only wanted his software (and only his software) to run on his devices. That provides another element of control over the perception of the overall design.

Jony Ive, the design genius at Apple, was interviewed in some depth and complained about companies such as Xiaomi copying Apple's design language[1]. Think about that in terms of the corporate theory. Apple could reasonably consider that its design talent has long been a resource that outperforms the competitors around it. Microsoft's iPod competitor, the Zune, didn't catch on, in part, because it was just not as attractive and easy to use. Lots of tablets came to the market to try to compete with the iPad but it was at least two years before they really started to be as cleverly designed and well thought out.

The cross-sight comes, in part, in the recognition of elements of the graphical user interface (GUI) work done at Xerox. That included the not insignificant contribution the Xerox Parc group made of inventing the mouse! This was a key element in Apple's products, but the GUI complemented the other assets at Jobs's-note, if decide to stick with Jobs' then change other mentions p28 and p76 and Apple's disposal perfectly.

So what are the big takeaways here?

- **What does the future hold?** There is a measure of crystal ball gazing required here but we're talking about the realm of classic strategic analysis with Porter's Five Forces, PEST analysis, etc. as a starting point.
- **Isolate what you are exceptional at or what is unique to you.** There is no point basing your future on something that can be imitated easily by your competitors. You're hoping for longer lasting advantage from your strategic options.

- **Benchmark against the competition.** Consider combinations of the opportunities and unique resources/skills that you have but do so while considering your competition. You'll spot if something you are considering is actually weaker than you would like and also perhaps spot a strong potential move from your competitors before they do!

Source

Zenger, T., 'What Is the Theory of Your Firm?', *Harvard Business Review*, June 2013

[1] www.forbes.com/sites/timworstall/2014/10/12/jony-ive-complains-but-we-actually-want-people-to-copy-apples-designs

See also

If you've started reading here then have a look back at Chapter 6 on disruption and Chapter 7 on hypercompetition. They'll provide a good understanding of why the approach to strategy has to be different to how it was in the past.

The next chapter will marry the concepts of competitive advantage with increased adaptability in an organization.

14 COMPETITIVE ADAPTABILITY THROUGH ADAPTABILITY

It's not the fittest that will survive— it's the most adaptable

Now that's Charles Darwin's words a little but the sentiment is spot on for businesses in turbulent environments.

This chapter will explain about some 'new' rules for producing competitive advantage. These rules are based on adaptability and derive from the four organizational capabilities that can foster rapid change in organizations.

Martin Reeves and Mike Deimler wrote in the *Harvard Business Review* about work done in Boston Consulting Group. That consultancy is behind the seminal Boston Box model used in marketing as well as strategy; and provides interesting thinking about how organizations can and should work.

In the face of increasingly harsh competition and the general erosion of the chance to differentiate, they ask some pretty tough questions about the status quo of strategic thinking.

Think about these questions...

- How can we use frameworks centred on market positioning or economies of scale when the company can move from leadership to being a follower from one year to the next?
- When the overlap between markets is so blurred (and, I'd add, changes so quickly), how can you even define market positioning and/or leadership?
- When there is so much information to consider, and of course this is only getting worse as we embrace the concepts of 'Big

Data', how do managers pick the right information they'll need to make good decisions?

- If change happens so fast, and new business models can undermine or kill existing ones ever more quickly, how can companies rely on a strategic process that might only happen once a year and which might even be trying to pin down a five-year period into the future?

Pretty brutal aren't they. If we accept that these are true, and let's face it they are absolutely on the money, the challenge is that things like economies of scale or a differentiated offering can no longer be considered guarantees of success into the future.

The researchers put the logical consequence of these observations really well. Rather than being good at one thing, you need to be good at learning how to do new things. And I'd amend that slightly by adding, 'and learning to be good at doing those new things!'.

The book *Who Moved My Cheese?* (see below) might be a slim read but it's based on this same idea. We get comfortable doing the same thing and expecting the same results. When that situation changes it's those that have remained vigilant for new sources of cheese that will find them, and that will probably be happier doing so. These ones are programmed for the search for the new cheese, not for consumption of the stuff that they wrongly hope will always be there.

So what are the four attributes that are necessary to explore new territories and boldly go where no company has gone before.

THE PATH TO ADAPTABILITY

Reading and acting on signs of change

So who is doing that and in what ways?

The data analysis firm behind the longer-term success at Tesco in the UK, dunnhumby, has 40 petabytes of data about who buys what, at which price points, from what stores, under which circumstances, etc. That's a lot of input to help Tesco make better decisions. A great article in *Forbes* magazine describes how American retailer Target was able to correlate purchases made by pregnant women and then use that data to actually predict both that a loyalty card holder was pregnant and even the expected due date, just from the pattern of purchases.

If you don't turn up to the gym for a while, they may send you emails encouraging you to come to classes or make you a special offer with a personal trainer. They know you've not been for a while, and they know that people who don't come are more likely to cancel their membership, and so they try to keep you. In fact, people that happily pay every month but never show up are great for them, but they don't want you to suddenly come to your senses, spot you are wasting money and leave.

Mobile phone companies need to look at your account history and your projected 'customer lifetime value' to them to understand how hard they should try to keep you as a customer. They also need to figure out who is at most risk of leaving by looking at past behaviours to identify indicators of potential churn to another provider. If they do this, and they get it right, they can target the high lifetime value customers that are relatively more likely to leave. By investing in these people with retention bonuses, discounted handsets, etc., they are reading the right signs and then acting in the right way.

If an organization is not reading signals, or does it worse than competitors and/or never does anything about them, then I fear for its longevity.

The ability to experiment rapidly

For those things you can't accurately predict or measure, then you'll need a mechanism for trying things out. The further down the route you get to actually launching a product, the more expensive it becomes.

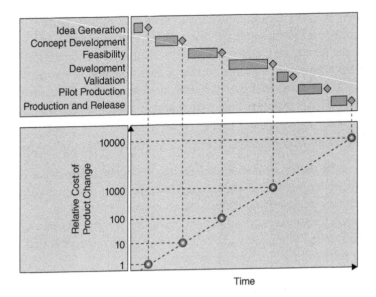

Figure 14.1 The cost of product change during the development life cycle

The diagram above represents how the cost of changing a product increases as it moves over time from an idea through development and on to production. The later you catch any bad choices or errors, the more costly it will be.

So ideally you want to cut bad ideas early (if you know they are bad), and only invest in winners. That's not a surprise but is harder to do than to discuss.

Orange, the French headquartered mobile phone operator, has GigaStudio (based in San Francisco) acting as a laboratory for new products and services that will take advantage of gigabit broadband services (or similar). That gives them the chance, potentially, to see winners early and exploit them before the competition. Also based in San Francisco is Orange Fab. This supports early stage start-ups. These are mechanisms for experimentation for them – not always using their own money, which is also rather smart.

Going back to dunnhumby for a moment, it can help Tesco reconfigure stores, move products around, change prices, etc. and see the results very quickly. Tesco can then revert if something doesn't work, or roll it out further across similar stores with similar buyer demographics, habits, preferences, etc. if the ideas work. This is fast experimentation and feedback in action.

The ability to manage complex systems of stakeholders

To really understand what is going on, an organization needs to use intelligence that is not just derived internally. For example, where an organization is drawing on external partners for design, manufacturing, fulfilment, customer service, customer care, technical support... then it's clearly going to be vital that it considers all parts of this ecosystem.

The successful 'adaptive company' will be integrating these different parties at a strategic level. Remember, some of these external companies will be common to the competitors also. However, it's about creating a unique or highly differentiated system that will help the company win.

This might mean a car manufacturer allowing suppliers to produce sub-assemblies rather than simply providing components. It might be the close integration of a supplier like ARM in the design of the processors Apple uses. These aren't arm's length relationships. These suppliers are then acting almost like business units of their customer's organizations.

The ability to motivate employees and partners

Adaptation is not something that can be done in the most rigid command and control structure. Decision-making has to be fast and fluid. That's not going to work where everything has to be raised further up the organization for a decision.

For service parts of an organization, such as the IT department, cleaning and facilities, then a hierarchical approach is fine. Where flexibility is required, an organization closer to a project matrix structure is going to be more appropriate. In that approach, the organization tries to pick the right mix of investments into programmes, select the best potential projects and then have people 'usefully busy' within the project teams. Interesting stuff but slightly tricky to get across in a few lines. Let's stick to the principles though and explain some more about this attribute.

As an example of how these ideas can be put in place, the authors quote Netflix and the nine core behaviours they believe are key for employees. These are:

- communication
- judgement
- courage
- innovation
- passion
- selflessness
- honesty
- curiosity
- impact.

Clear, consistent and unambiguous right?

To fully embrace the idea of becoming an adaptive company, the team suggests there are some simple things you should ensure are happening.

Look at what maverick companies are doing. Move the focus away from purely looking at the traditional competitors and on to fast movers, new players and those with unusual approaches.

Spot uncertainties and address them.

Address every risk. In part this should address the point above. You should have things going on in the company to address every significant risk and uncertainty. Look at them now. Understand the potential impact and avoid/mitigate the downsides before they become crises. Alternatively, some of these will give rise to opportunities that you won't want to miss.

Examine multiple alternatives. This will require more work but look for a greater number of strategic or change-related alternatives to make better decisions and avoid having only one proposal for a given situation.

Increase the clock speed. That's a phrase from electronics where each instruction happens on a tick from a clock. If you make that clock tick more quickly, the instructions happen faster. Same with the company, let's think about faster everything. Not to the extent that huge mistakes start to be made, but also accept that by going faster you will make some errors.

Consider if your market is so stable that you don't need to become more adaptive. However, for most organizations, this thinking is important. Use the headings in this chapter as a checklist.

So what are the big takeaways here?

- **Mind the gap!** Measure where you are out of ten today (where ten is excellent) for each attribute. This will help to identify where you could improve and also where a lower score may be okay for now. To be clear, companies do not necessarily need to be excellent for every attribute.
- **Are we going too slowly and thinking too comfortably?** In corporate terms, have you got fat and lazy? Think about which fast-moving companies or trends are going to hurt you. Which companies will exploit clever new business models first – you or the competition?
- **Today's market-leading situation will not last.** As Reeves and Deimler point out, if economies of scale and market leadership were enough, Nokia would still 'own' the smartphone market. Instead, the phone division was bought by Microsoft and they have killed the Nokia phone branding.

Source

Reeves. M. & Deimler. M., 'Adaptability: The New Competitive Advantage In a world of constant change, the spoils go to the nimble'. *Harvard Business Review*, July 2011

See also

The next chapter throws in a real twist to the concept of competitive advantage. It suggests that your current advantages may make you blind to the need to adapt these or even find new ones for the future. It doesn't suggest that competitive advantage is dead for all companies and markets, but I think the chapter is completely correct in that for many industries a sustainable competitive advantage will be increasingly difficult to achieve.

Chapter 22 – Talks about how to deal with shifting environments.

Chapter 9 – Discusses how to exploit disruption.

Further reading

Johnson, Spencer, *Who Moved My Cheese?* (G. P. Putnam's Sons, New York, 1998)

McGrath, Rita Gunther, *The End of Competitive Advantage* (Harvard Business Review Press, Boston, 2013)

15 WHY STOPPING IS AS IMPORTANT AS STARTING

The end of competitive advantage?!

Okay that statement may seem inconsistent with some of the earlier chapters. For example, Chapter 12 outlined the concept of competitive advantage and strategic thinkers from Michael E. Porter to Kenichi Ohmae have all stressed the need for sustainability in how you compete. Who would invest heavily in an advantage that only lasted a short while? So what are we talking about?

Rita Gunther McGrath is a professor at Columbia Business School and focuses on strategy and innovation in today's challenging environment for businesses. Her research has looked at the mechanisms for competition and how organizations fail. From 2010 her team identified companies with a market capitalization of more than US$1 billion and identified those that had been able to grow revenue by 5 per cent for each of the previous five years. During that period, the growth in GDP was around 4 per cent and so these companies were outperforming the national economy in terms of their growth.

The team found only 8 per cent of companies were above this 5 per cent growth threshold and a repeat of the work for the period from 2000 to 2004 was similarly disappointing, highlighting only 15 per cent of firms.

Finally, the team honed in on the companies that had been able to achieve that 5 per cent revenue growth year in, year out over the ten-year period to 2009. The answer? Just ten!

The work then considered the three main competitors for each of these special ten companies and also compared them to one another. The results were surprising.

A key finding was that these companies had long-term perspectives on where they wanted to get to but, more importantly, they recognized that what they are doing today will not deliver future growth. Think about that for a second. They're saying that no matter how good their advantages in the market today, that's not going to be enough for the future.

There are two parts to this recognition.

First, it's a rational response to the way that competitive environments are changing for many companies. De Beers may still dig little rocks out of the ground, polish them a bit and sell them, but many companies do not have the luxury and stability of De Beers' dominance in diamond production. We talk about 'high-velocity' companies where the speed of change is very fast and stability hard to obtain. The environment around some companies has changed so radically that the idea of creating and maintaining a sustainable competitive advantage may be unattainable.

Second, the important realization for these companies is that you cannot sit back. You cannot rest on whatever position you have achieved today because the world will change around you and you need to change with it.

Being the greatest manufacturer of steam trains was a fantastic market position at one time but the introduction of diesel engines changed the market completely.

Skype becomes the dominant player for international calls

Telecom operators used to make huge revenues from international phone calls. The call would need to be routed across the originator's network to an international gateway from where it might cross oceans in dedicated undersea cables or span the globe using satellites. Eventually it would be routed across the copper wire network in the destination country and the call established. Each leg of this call's journey and every country crossed would increase the costs. Twenty years ago, many telecoms companies were monopolies and they could charge what they wished in the absence of any real competition – enabling them to make good profits on these calls.

The spread of access to the Internet has now changed the market forever. Companies such as BT were looking at transferring calls across the Internet in the early 2000s but looked at this approach as an opportunity to reduce their own internal costs. They did not see it as something that could be used by a completely new entrant to disrupt their core business in the way it eventually would.

Skype was introduced in 2003 as a way to make free calls between PCs, but the opportunity to make a call from a PC and transfer the call around the world on the Internet was quickly identified. Rather than paying the significant transit costs for a call over satellite or passing through copper wires in the ground, these calls would only incur a small charge in the destination country where they leave the Internet and essentially become a local call.

The result was the extraordinary growth in the use of Skype, with 24.7 per cent of global international call minutes being carried over Skype in 2011 (up from 12 per cent in 2009)[1]. In parallel, Skype-to-Skype calls grew 48 per cent in 2011 and reached a total of 145 billion minutes, with 40 per cent of those calls including video[2].

The number of users and the potential to dominate the market led to the high valuations of Skype in the purchase by eBay for £1.4 billion in 2005[3] and subsequently by Microsoft for £5.2 billion in 2011[4].

Skype's entry into the market has both taken away significant market share from the traditional telco players and also driven down prices so far that customers are now paying just 1-2 per cent of the price they used to pay for international calls.

DEVELOPING A NEW CORPORATE MINDSET

Rita Gunther McGrath talks about a number of changes that can be made to the mindset of the business to help it be more nimble and flexible in the future. Let's be very clear about this. It means a change in culture is likely to be needed.

Considering theories and experience in delivering change projects in the past, this type of change, a Theory O[5] (for organization) type project, is not one that can be done quickly. This may involve changes to processes, metrics and support systems, but it will also likely need a redefinition of roles and responsibilities and the organizational structure that underpins these. Finally, the skills of individuals may need to be improved and/or new employees found to better match the required approach. This isn't something that takes weeks or even months. It may take years to reconfigure a business.

That means you need to start this type of evolution/revolution well before the business indicators start to become a problem. This also means that it may be trickier to justify as any change is harder when things are going right. However, if you don't start early enough, the business will not be immune when things change around it.

As a first step to this type of change, look at the following and consider how your organization is currently configured compared to the industry you are in. If that industry is very stable (e.g. oil and gas), then the urgency for change will be less strong than in other sectors. Otherwise, you can quickly audit where you think the organization is today between the two positions.

Where you are...	Where you need to be...
Assuming current advantages will remain	Assuming current advantages will come under pressure
Conversations/work that confirms your current perspectives	Conversations that challenge the status quo
Relatively few people involved in developing strategy (and with a narrow perspective)	Broader constituencies involved in strategy process with a wide range of perspectives

Search for precise answers but slow	Fast and roughly right
Prediction focus	Discovery focus
Focus on Net Present Value (the financial return of a particular project)	Focus on providing options
Focus on optimization	Focus on the external environment
People aimed at solving problems	People aimed at identifying and exploiting new opportunities
Focus on prolonging the current model	Focus on accepting the need for, and finding continual shifts
Accepting a slow decline/death	Finding a new fight

Also consider how you are positioned relative to your strongest competitors. If they are better positioned than you then you may need to catch up – fast! However, a comfortable lead against your traditional competition mustn't lull you into a false sense of security. In today's business climate, the threat can come from anywhere and just watching your current competitors won't help you against tomorrow's new entrants.

So what are the big takeaways here?

- **Don't wait until it's too late.** Start thinking about how to move your organization today. Look at the table above and work out what you can enact by forcing yourselves to be more like the right-hand column, until it becomes a natural embedded part of the business.
- **Sweat the small stuff. It might not be small forever.** Keep questioning: 'How long have we got until we need to change?', 'Can we afford to wait?', 'What are the early indicators that our current advantages are being eroded?'
- **Fake it until you can make it.** The concept that 'Sustainable Competitive Advantage is Dead' will be true for many companies – even if they haven't realized it yet. Even if it's not true for your company or industry today, you should always act as if it's true for you, and configure your business to continually evolve the way in which you compete. Build

the questions about losing competitive advantage into your management approach to identify (and hopefully respond to) fading competitive advantage before it is too late.

Sources

Beer, M. and Nohria N., 'Cracking the code of change', *Harvard Business Review*, May-June 2000

McGrath, Rita Gunther, *The End of Competitive Advantage* (Harvard Business Review Press, Boston, 2013)

See also

The next chapter will address some keys to building a strategy 'playbook' that will structure an approach to not just identifying fading competitive advantage, but building an organization that moves flexibly to reconfigure itself and its offerings to the market.

To explore this concept in more detail, read 'Picking which competitive advantage to pursue', Chapter 12, and Chapter 14 on competitive advantage through adaptability.

Notes

[1] Samer Abu Latif, General Manager – Gulf, Microsoft. Speech at Broadband World Forum 2012 – Dubai

[2] Telegeography.com January 2012

[3] BBC news report, 12 September 2005

[4] BBC news report, 10 May 2011

[5] Beer, M. and Nohria N., 'Cracking the code of change', *Harvard Business Review*, May-June 2000

16 MARKETING AS STRATEGY

Thinking beyond products and services

Niraj Dawar is a professor at Ivey Business School in Ontario. He wrote a really interesting book, *Tilt: Shifting your strategy from products to customers.*

His work suggests that companies should understand that the main strategic question has moved on. It's no longer, 'what else can we make?', instead, companies should ask: 'what else can we do for our customers?'

Dawar uses a really simple example we can all relate to – soft drinks. A can of Pepsi Max may cost less than 50p in a supermarket. At Stockholm's Arlanda Airport I recently paid the equivalent of more than three pounds. Trapped on a budget airline flight on the way home, I paid even more for a lukewarm can so small it wouldn't have satisfied a slightly thirsty mouse. It's not just about the product/service – it's about the context.

A different example would be Uber. The company doesn't have any taxis but they arrange for private individuals to give lifts to people who pay the drivers and, of course, Uber makes a cut. However, Uber realized that there were lots of unhappy clients at certain times of peak demand. Their answer has been described by them as 'economics 101' (or completely sensible business practice). At times of peak demand, the price goes up for a ride. Not a huge surprise but we're not talking about a 10 per cent increase. We're talking up to seven times the standard price! So a ride (I won't say taxi ride as they have explained how they are absolutely not a taxi service) is not always a ride!

Dawar suggests that in the case of a can of cola, the extra value that justifies the additional price over the 'cost' of the can, is the convenience provided. Someone doesn't need to remember to buy cola at the supermarket or, in my case, to carry multiple cans onto a plane.

He observes that most businesses are still focused around the older concepts of a product and production focus. As he correctly points out, the ideas of striving for efficiency and economies of scale are great but, when everyone is doing the same thing, it becomes hard to use these activities to drive differentiation. So it's the downstream activities that will increasingly be important.

So let's repeat that shift in thinking mentioned above. We need to move away from 'what else can we make?' to 'what else can we do for our customers?'.

The change this brings is that customers are central to the company's thinking. Now you could argue that this is always the case but it's that important difference that you're thinking beyond a product or service to identify all the things that could be done for a customer. If you're face down in taking 0.01 per cent off the cost of a widget, or making it 10 g lighter then it's easy to forget all the other experiential, buying occasion and usage-related stuff, etc.

The challenge with these downstream sources of competitive advantage is that they involve parties that are external to the organization. This might mean from the many channels to market, through companies that complement the organization through to the company's customers themselves.

UPSTREAM ACTIVITIES				DOWNSTREAM ACTIVITIES		
Sourcing	Production	Logistics	Innovation	Shaping Customer Perception	Innovation	Building Cumulative Advantage
Contract with lowest cost suppliers	Reduce costs, maximise economies of scale, improve efficiency, reduce wastage, improve quality (if appropriate)	Optimise supply chain Efficient and timely deliveries Just in time concepts	Build better products or similar ones more cheaply Find new ways to deliver functionality Look for new solutions		Customise offerings to match the situation for consumption Reduce customer costs Reduce customer risks	Accrue effects from the network Accrue and use customer data
Fixed costs, customer value and competitive advantage moving downstream						

Figure 16.1 Upstream and downstream sources of competitive advantage

Reprinted by permission of Harvard Business Review. From *Tilt: Shifting Your Strategy from Products to Customers* by Dawar, Niraj, 2013. Copyright © 2013 by Harvard Business Publishing; all rights reserved

So let's get to the fundamentals of who should apply this thinking. Dawar suggests the following types of companies will find this thinking particularly valuable:

- **Product-obsessed industries** (e.g. mobile phones)
- **Companies in industries that are approaching (or in) maturity.** At this point in the product life-cycle, a company can spend on advertising, etc. to try to get brand switchers from competitors but finding advantages that are not easy to copy is very important to them.
- **Companies trying to move up the value chain.** These companies are looking for sustainable sources of value creation and/or competitive advantage.

GOING BEYOND A NEW PRODUCT OR SERVICE

Dawar uses his thinking to discuss some interesting and somewhat counterintuitive thoughts.

Listening to customers or not?

Dawar quotes feedback from Steve Jobs about the market research that went into the iPad development. His snappy comeback was that there was none, adding that it's not up to the customer to know what they want!

The classic older version of this approach comes from Henry Ford. His view was that, if asked, his customers would not have asked for the Model T, they'd have asked for a faster horse!

We talk about Zara's ultra-fast production cycle elsewhere in this book (Chapter 26). However, from a marketing perspective, the important factor of what the company does is that it gets new designs on the shelves quickly and then responds to real purchase behaviour. I always think the ultimate arbiter of customer opinion is whether they pay for the stuff with their own money. Zara is doing real world, real money market research using the shelves in its stores – and not focus groups.

Dawar's not saying ignore your customers but he is strongly suggesting you need to define what performance really means in your particular sector. You set an agenda around what you do for the customer, not just tightly defining a customer need.

Will competitive advantage erode over time?

Welcome to the only chapter in this book that fights against the idea that advantages erode – Dawar says no (well not always). In fact, whichever view is right, I believe you should act as if competitive advantage will be fleeting as it will keep you sharp and alert to new opportunities for yourself, or where you need to head off the competition.

However, Dawar discusses the cumulative effect for companies that compete downstream. I'd cite WhatsApp as a great example of this. It had 5 per cent of the world's messaging market at a time when there were only around 24 people in the company. However, if you wanted to compete with them, you'd need to get the millions and millions of users they had on their platform. If you had WhatsApp then you didn't need anything else. The greater the number of users, the greater this downstream advantage for every other user. This is a network effect in action.

An alternative mechanism here is to simply gather and use data better than your competition. That may be more data or just better uses, but you're looking for wisdom that comes from that data. Amazon can use the huge swathes of buying data to predict future purchases and also make recommendations to customers. They are also looking at predictive delivery approaches where they deliver items closer to customers to provide for fast delivery when customers actually order them. That's not quite shipping it to the door before you realize you want something but it's moving towards that.

Who else has that data? Who else can use their own shipping data as well as Amazon to optimize delivery processes, locations, etc.? You should be thinking about this in your ecosystem. It affects all parts of the value chain but the downstream parts are definitely enhanced by wise use of their data.

Choose your competitors?

Dawar provides the great example of Brita. It positions its water filters in the bottled water aisle. There, the filters represent a way to get more 'pure' water per buck than the large and cumbersome bottles.

Price is also a very strong indicator of who you compete with (in the mind of your customers).

Robinsons has been making squash for decades. However, it first moved to a double concentrate version (increasing convenience) before a super-concentrated version that is small but can still make 20 drinks when you add water. The concept is it's in your bag for when you want a drink. Now apart from the need to have a source of water, this product is competing with soft drinks, bars, vending machines, etc. It's no longer competing with other makers of squash! Well not until they copy the concept (and a few already have). It was an advantage but wasn't sustainable for that long.

Does innovation always relate to technology?

Well think about Apple. I get people saying I should abandon a lifetime of Microsoft products and start using Apple. But when I looked at an ultrabook purchase, the difference between the actual stuff under the hood in a MacBook Air (MBA) and a few ultrabooks was very small. Windows 8 does most things pretty well and no it's not IOS X but it's fine. However, the MacBook was around £300 more. Why would I pay that? Well the answer for some is the positioning of Apple as the 'outsider' brand. A MacBook Air is not a product from the empire of Microsoft but is seen as a user-friendly device from the 'cool kids'. They're not competing on RAM or processor or those mundane things that ultrabooks use to try to outstrip one another in the market. Apple is competing on other things entirely.

So what are the big takeaways here?

What to do?

- **As Nike might say about this approach, Just Do It!** Shift thinking towards 'what else can we do for our customers'. That's not just more products/services (although that shouldn't be off the table). This is particularly referring to enhancing the customer consumption experience, etc. (the 'augmented product' as marketeers would call it).
- **Ask, ask and ask again.** How are we going to improve the overall choice, experience, consistency, location, etc. of consumption of our product? It really is such an important (and simple) concept that it must be part of any approach to strategy.

Source

Dawar, Niraj, *Tilt: Shifting Your Strategy from Products to Customers* (Harvard Business Review Press, Boston, 2013)

See also

Chapters 14 and 15 – Consider aspects of competitive advantage.

17 UNDERSTANDING YOUR MARKET SITUATION

You need to know where you are before you decide how to get where you want to go

A key stage in deciding what strategies might work is to look at what is happening in your own market. PEST analysis helps understand the external influences on a market (Political, Economic, Social, Technological, Legal, Environmental, Demographic, etc.). Beyond that, the Porter's Five Forces Model is a good next step – simple but effective.

Michael Porter has developed more influential business models than probably anyone on the planet. The strength of this one is that it makes you look hard at every type of player in the market, rather than becoming obsessed with one aspect.

The model shows that a company is influenced by a number of things. First we will consider the actions of competitors in their chosen markets.

The vertical axis shows how the competitive balance can be altered by new players entering the market or products/services acting as substitutes for the customer's money.

The horizontal axis reflects how the other players in the supply chain can exert their power to influence the situation.

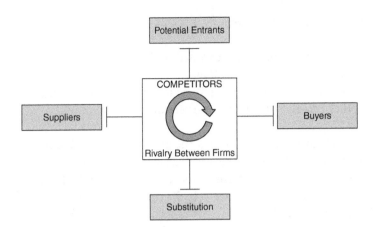

Figure 17.1 The Five Forces Model

The Five Forces therefore represent the competitive rivalry with the four other major power influences – buyers, suppliers, potential entrants into the market and the potential for substitution.

Competitive rivalry

Competitive rivalry will be affected by many factors including:

- number and size of competitors
- market share
- maturity of the market
- costs to exit the market (this could be financial but could also be loss of face, keeping the company in a market it should really leave)
- profit margins
- cash flow
- capacity utilization
- strategies and ambitions.

Buyer power

This is the amount of power that buyers can exert on an organization with regard to the price they pay, terms they will agree to, service agreements and specifications.

The power is higher when:

- the buying group is concentrated (only a few buyers)
- purchases are made in volume
- the purchase doesn't save money for the buyer or provide any other perceived value (i.e. is essentially a commodity).

A potato farmer might find that the pool of buyers has reduced over time with local greengrocers closing down in the face of competition from supermarkets. The farmer may find that those same supermarkets are actually their only potential buyer – limiting the farmer's power to negotiate and allowing supermarkets to aggressively dictate their own terms.

Supplier power

This is the power that suppliers have in negotiating terms and conditions with the potential purchaser. This is about the balance between a supplier's ability to drive prices up against the buyer's ability to change supplier.

Suppliers are more powerful when:

- The product/service is highly differentiated
- The costs to switch to an alternative are high (e.g. in the car industry where a part may be designed for a seven-year life and switching may mean safety tests have to be re-done or require re-design of other components)
- The market is not important to the supplier (e.g. low margins or turnover)
- There is no competition or only few competitors
- They could enter the market of the companies buying from them (this threat of entry makes it harder for buyers to exert much power on suppliers).

Let's look in more depth at the case of two competitors in a market as it illustrates some interesting thinking about how they might behave.

Duopolies

As a rule of thumb, two companies in a market does not create true competition. It creates a duopoly. If there is potential to differentiate the products in some way then one company may be able to outperform its competitor. However, there are also several ways in which a form of equilibrium can occur between the two.

- If the product is nearer to being a true commodity with little differentiation between products then a natural equilibrium may occur where performance is broadly similar (e.g. Mastercard and Visa).
- The smaller company may undercut the prices of its larger competitor by a certain amount, but there is then a danger of entering a price war that it would almost certainly lose.

The end result can be that even without any formal discussions between the two about fixing pricing (since this would be illegal), the situation can stabilize with the large company 'allowing' the smaller one to exist and the smaller one accepting that actions to increase its market share might not be a good idea.

There are, of course, exceptions. The fight between Boeing and Airbus illustrates that sometimes two competitors do go all out in the same market.

Threats from potential new entrants into the market

This threat relates to the ability for new players to credibly enter and disrupt the market. In particular, this forces a company to consider the barriers to entry that exist (or could be erected) to prevent another company entering their market.

Potential for substitution

Substitution means satisfying the same customer need in a different way.

Netflix and Amazon Instant Video are alternatives to buying a TV or film series on DVD. However so is pirated content. Now you might say that's illegal and you're right! However, that doesn't stop people doing it and you must always consider all the potential substitutes facing you – not just the legal ones.

A summer holiday might be replaced by a skiing break in winter. However, the money earmarked for the holiday could equally be used to pay for a new bathroom, a motorbike or anything else the buyer wants. Where the spending is on something that is 'nice to have' rather than a 'must-have', then it's difficult to predict exactly where the money might go.

UNDERSTANDING THE POWER OF DIFFERENT PLAYERS IN YOUR CURRENT ENVIRONMENT

Five Forces should be a staple part of a strategic assessment. Alongside PEST analysis it provides a simple and structured approach to figuring out where you are.

There are some practical points to remember in using it.

Far too often, I've seen the 'competitors' section become a listing of the competition. That's not really very helpful and doesn't tell you much. The content relating to competition should actually be about what they are doing that is making life easier or harder for you. New products, special offers, improved terms, people leaving the market, people joining the market – everything that is impacting your bottom line needs to be considered.

In using this model and PEST analysis, people sometimes get confused about which category things might fit into. The simple answer is don't worry about that. The important thing is get the facts down on paper somewhere and do something about them. There are no prizes for having something in the right box. There are big prizes (like growth, better margins or even plain old survival) for spotting what's important to your situation and doing the right thing in response.

One category that needs some care is thinking about buyers. For FMCG companies, they don't sell directly to consumers in most cases. You can't order Pepsi Max direct from Pepsi (sadly). So when they consider their customers, they could limit their thinking to supermarkets, wholesalers, etc. and completely forget their end customers. However, they are way too smart for that. They will also consider the end consumers of the product and what is happening in their world. This means that for many companies, you have to consider a two-stage process where you look at your direct customers and also the people that they sell to.

This is critical. If your direct customer is in trouble, then you're in trouble. However if they're fine but the number of their customers is dwindling, or they have less available cash or any other problem, again their troubles are your troubles!

In terms of potential entrants, there are two concepts that can help you identify who might join your market. The first is to look across your suppliers and others in the value chain. They might decide to get in on the action in the future. In mobile handsets, new suppliers like Oppo and OnePlus have entered the market among manufacturers spotting that their expertise in creating handsets for others could equally well be used to make models for themselves.

So what are the big takeaways here?

- **It may not be perfect but Five Forces is a must-do exercise.** It's not perfect but it should be compulsory. You'll always learn something so you should always do this as part of a structured exercise that includes PEST analysis. By doing the two together you reduce the chances of missing something. If you forget some aspect of the spending power of buyers, it might be captured under the Economic category in PEST. Between the two models, you should be able to cover the big areas affecting your environment and market.
- **Avoid taking a static view.** The business situation is not a painting. Things are evolving, so think about what is changing that will affect the way you do business and change those in your ecosystem.
- **Identifying your situation is not the same as changing it.** Doing this analysis only counts if you make the changes that it helps you identify. If not, you've wasted your time doing it.

Source

Porter, Michael E., *Competitive Strategy: Techniques for Analyzing Industries and Competitors* (The Free Press, New York, 2004)

See also

Chapter 18 – Seeks to extend Porter's thinking to consider how more dynamic competitive markets can be understood and exploited.

Chapter 22 – Provides a useful counterpoint to this chapter and questions how far you should rely on classic models such as Five Forces.

Further reading

Johnson, Gerry, Scholes, Kevan & Whittington, Richard, *Exploring Corporate Strategy* (FT/Prentice Hall, Harlow, 2007)

Porter, Michael E., *Competitive Advantage* (The Free Press, Cambridge, 2004)

18 THE NEW DYNAMICS OF COMPETITION

Beyond Five Forces into a new model of business relationships

This chapter takes Porter's classic thinking and discusses the more complex relationships that occur in sharing value between the different players in a value 'system'.

This may be the only chapter of its type in the book as it does not represent definitive work. It's more of a work in progress, but is so fascinating that I think it is well worth including.

Michael Ryall begins his thinking with an interesting reminder of the later Peter Drucker's views on innovation. Drucker talked of the anticipation of an impending innovation happening for a while before it finally hits and kicks off a huge amount of change. Companies will be fighting the innovation, suffering because of it, changing to exploit it, new players will be emerging, etc. This will carry on through the classic growth phase of the product life-cycle before the 'shake out' phase, where the number of players will reduce as some abandon the market and others combine their efforts.

These innovations appear from what consultants sometimes call 'technology intercepts'. These occur where price, performance, quality, availability, acceptability or other factors evolve over time and eventually combine to push something from a 'no' to a 'yes' in the market. Something becomes cheap enough, small enough, good enough, etc.

Chapter 17 discussed the Five Forces model from Michael Porter. It's a very important model and to make sense of this chapter, it will help if you've read Chapter 17 first. Go on. I'll be here waiting.

Ryall's work is grounded in Porter's model but discusses some evolutionary steps in thinking that followed Porter's work.

His first concern is that the thinking that followed the development of Porter's Five Forces approach failed to put in place a rigorous set of thinking that could correlate company performance with any of the fundamental variables in the business. It was useful to help illustrate points of view but it failed to really apply the rigour that was needed. Ryall perhaps cheekily calls this 'In Search of Excellence' syndrome – pointing at Peters and Waterman's management smash-hit book of the same name that hailed the performance of a number of companies, most of which failed in the mid-term. Ryall wants more than theories and anecdotes – he wants rigour and correlations and cites the excellent, 'Value-Based Business Strategy', by Adam M. Brandenburger and Harborne W. Stuart Jr.

They defined value creation as:

willingness to pay (the peak price a buyer is willing to pay for a product/service – above which the buyer considers it is better not to have it)

less

the opportunity cost (this is the lowest price a supplier will take and still be willing to supply the goods to the company).

These may be slightly confusing so think about the simple fundamentals. If a buyer has a cheaper alternative, they will not buy from you (generally). If the cost savings your product can provide are less than the purchase price then you'll see the same result (assuming that it is an important purchasing factor). On the supplier side, if a company can secure a higher price for their goods or services from someone else – they will!

Brandenburger and Stuart looked at a number of elements that constituted a 'successful' approach in their minds.

First, they recognize that value is not just created in the organization – it should be considered more externally with an emphasis on buyers and suppliers.

The importance of suppliers is key to their thinking since they view that too many strategies seek to satisfy customers but do not go beyond this to think about how supplier relationships can generate (or destroy) value. This aspect of managing suppliers can be as limited as an over-focus on cost cutting.

The third aspect of their thinking is the idea of cooperative game theory, as opposed to non-cooperative game theory... obviously. The latter requires a degree of thinking about chess moves into the future that would give most of us a headache. The cooperative theory is much less structured and allows for a variety of situations. Think of it as competitive dynamics.

GOING BEYOND CLASSIC STRATEGIC MODELS

Brandenburger and Stuart came up with four value-based strategies all based around the creation of favourable asymmetries between a company and its competitors. The four boxes show what the firm should do with regard to the customer and suppliers and the different factors.

	Firm	Competitors
Willingness to pay	Classic differentiation strategies to raise the willingness to pay for your products/ services.	Lower customers' willingness to pay for competitors' products. E.g. set up switching costs that make it more expensive to change to them. Moving from Xbox to PS4 requires buying a new console. Changing razor systems from Gillette to Wilkinson means buying an expensive handle first rather than simply more 'relatively' inexpensive heads.

Opportunity cost	Lower the cost of suppliers doing business with the company. E.g. lower the cost for the supplier to deliver to the firm – larger orders, greater delivery flexibility (so they produce for you during slack times), etc.	Increase the cost for suppliers to deliver to other providers (or make it impossible). E.g. exclusivity deals, contracts specifying 'most favoured nation' status so that you get the best deal from them.

Classic marketing/strategic theory is really only shown in the top left box, while the other three are often glossed over or ignored completely in an over-focusing on the company's own situation.

Ryall takes this work further towards an approach he calls the 'Value Capture Model'.

In this, an elegant simplicity emerges compared to the tensions in the Five Forces Model. In every relationship (suppliers, buyers, etc.), the competition works in both directions. The company competes for suppliers and vice versa. The company fights for customers and vice versa.

So which customers are fighting for products/services?

- In 2014, serious undersupply of the OnePlus One smartphone led to forums full of anxious potential customers and massive over-subscription in a one-hour pre-registration offer.
- Uber customers are fighting for taxis, and paying up to 7 times the base price to get one at times of very high demand.
- Concert goers 'compete' to get tickets for a hot show or concert – getting online at a set time and hoping they'll get to the front of the queue before the tickets are sold out.

This creates a force in each area, based on the intensity of that completion. The greater the number and attractiveness of alternative ways of gaining value to a party, the greater the intensity and tension in the relationship.

Ryall shows the burgeoning area of value capture models as a network of the relationships between the different parties (existing and potential).

The value network maps he creates show how the company, its suppliers and its customers combine to generate a given amount of value. The second part is then how different players appropriate this value. This is limited by the players who are currently outside the situation – in the 'competitive periphery' as he puts it. If there are other suppliers who wish to transact with you but aren't at the moment, this improves your position as the current suppliers' position is weakened. If you can find other customers for your product/services, and these are not currently serviced, the strength of your current customers is similarly diminished.

In moving from the VCM to thinking about strategic options, Ryall considers two types of investments in resources and capabilities.

The first is around influencing actual or potential value. These have **competitive intent** as they will help you do better than your competitors. Advertising is an example of this, increasing the maximum capturable value the firm could achieve.

The second concept is around investments in resources and capabilities to help persuade third parties transacting with the company to give up value – above what competitive logic would dictate is necessary. This is about **persuasive intent**.

So what are the big takeaways here?

- **Look beyond the boundaries of the Five Forces model.** The core relationships are correctly defined but the supplier and buyer relationships flow both ways. However, you also need to think about competitors' relationships with those two to help find interesting new approaches.

- **Thinking win-lose doesn't work anymore.** You have to find the right way to maximize the value created and then get as much as you can but leave enough for other players (e.g. suppliers). How 'friendly' you are on that will depend on how unique they are and also how unique you are to them.
- **Lock customers and suppliers in (if you can).** Helping suppliers reduce their costs in dealing with you will improve their stickiness to you, while creating barriers to switching is important in creating serious customer retention.

Sources

Brandenburger. A. M. & Stuart, H. W. Jr. (1996) [http://onlinelibrary.wiley.com/doi/10.1111/j.1430-9134.1996.00005.x/abstract], (2012), 'Value-Based Business Strategy', *Journal of Economics & Management Strategy*, Vol. 5 Issue 1 pp 5–24

Ryall, M. D., 'The New Dynamics of Competition – An emerging science for modeling strategic moves', *Harvard Business Review*, June [https://hbr.org/archive-toc/BR1306] 2013

See also

Chapter 12 – Discusses classic thinking about sources of competitive advantage and choices you can make...

Chapter 22 – Is similar but moves on to a discussion of what these choices mean to the company.

The next chapter introduces some great thinking about spotting when your business model is starting to hit trouble. Early warning is always good – then at least you have a chance to do something about it.

Further reading

Porter, Michael E., *Competitive Advantage* (The Free Press, Cambridge, 2004)

19 HOW TO AVOID YOUR BUSINESS MODEL GETTING INTO TROUBLE

Respond to signals before it's too late

The first thing here before we start worrying about a business model is to remind ourselves what that includes.

Essentially a business model describes the way in which your company does business. That means it includes the way in which it sets itself up in terms of customers, locations, sales channels, internal processes, technology, etc.

By now I think we've established the fact that business models are under threat from all sides and the attacks come faster than ever before. So it's clear we need to identify and respond to threats in the right way.

German general Helmuth von Moltke suggested that 'no battle plan survives first contact with the enemy' and boxer Mike Tyson, in a similar vein, said, 'everyone has a plan until they get hit'. No business model remains appropriate or effective forever. The art is in trying to see when a particular model is coming under threat.

This threat may be from many quarters. For example, it may be a crushing new technology that will change things very quickly but it could equally be a slow change in customer preferences. The chapters on identifying potential disruptions (and surviving them) are focused on looking for significant step changes but there is still potential for a business to die slowly.

So within an industry, we need to be more vigilant and do so in the face of shifting competition.

Rita Gunther McGrath writes about this in her book *The End of Competitive Advantage*.

The first part of this relates to the ability of companies to imitate a new product or service more quickly. This means that it's harder to get a lead in a market and maintain a leadership position.

The second part of this complexity is that we're seeing new entrants or approaches radically changing how markets work. For example, the smartphone is a great product 'killer' with serious impacts on products from cameras to satellite navigation devices. Consider your smartphone for a second. This assumes you have one. If you don't, I suggest you put the book down, go and buy one and then continue reading.

The sources of innovation and differentiation for these phones are becoming harder to find. Increasing screen size, screen resolution and camera functionality were all effective ways to compete for a while. However, most phones on the market now are pretty big, have a screen with better resolution than the human eye can resolve and a decent camera. As these features become increasingly similar across different phones, it becomes harder to come up with a 'hero' phone. The latest phones have tried water and dust proofing in order to be a bit different but we are now seeing the commoditization of this market with big, fast phones appearing at prices well below those targeted by Samsung, HTC, Sony and Apple. This is the essence of Kano analysis – watching as features start off as 'delighters' but then evolve to simply be 'basic needs' that every product needs to have to compete.

The third aspect of the complexity discussed by Rita Gunther McGrath is competition from companies offering an enhanced experience for customers above and beyond the basic product.

She cites Build-a-Bear as an example of this – where children (okay the parents love it too) build a more customized teddy bear for themselves, rather than just buying one off the shelf.

It's not enough to just consider the causes though. She identified three signs to detect when your model is in trouble.

Sign one

The first sign that your business model is starting to hit the difficulties that she discusses is a slowing in the rate of improvement. For example, if you are focused on cost reduction, then you may be starting to struggle to find the next potential saving. If this is the case, your competition may be following your path and soon be able to match your underlying cost structure. Alternatively, it may be that it becomes harder to think of new features to further enhance products/services.

Sign two

A second sign for concern is that customers are becoming happier with alternative offerings, or at the very least are prepared to try them.

Companies offering DVD rentals were not, initially, too concerned about the risk of online streaming. However, as broadband speeds improved, people found it increasingly easy to download video content. From a poor quality, low resolution product, improvements lead to more users downloading and eventually pretty much destroying the DVD rental market. There would have been only a subtle shift between the two methods of viewing content but it undermined many business models when it happened.

So Netflix all but kills Blockbuster video – but also illegal downloading became possible with faster broadband and so it also hurt the content providers (e.g. Sony, MGM, Universal, etc.) as it made it even easier to share their films and TV programmes.

Sign three

The final sign is when one or both of the above issues kick in and you then see the financials or other key performance indicators start to go south. Remember when this happens, these indicators do not tell you why they are happening. You're just seeing the logical consequence of how the company makes money being eroded over time.

SPOTTING YOUR BUSINESS MODEL IS IN TROUBLE

If your core business model is veering towards trouble, you need to identify alternatives. That sounds pretty simple doesn't it?

In reality, all of the methods in the book ask you to think about your company's position and strategy – or how you define new ones. This section could therefore simply point to any number of other chapters in the book. However, let's consider some of the indicators above and suggest what a business should be doing to spot trouble coming.

In simple terms, Rita Gunther McGrath highlights some indicators for companies that might indicate that their present sources of competitive advantage are being eroded. Stop and think for a second and see which ones might apply to your own organization:

- Do you 'eat your own dog food' as they say? If appropriate, then whether you are buying your own products/services becomes a significant question.
- Are returns on investment flat or falling?
- Do customers consider cheaper or simpler alternatives to be satisfactory for their needs?
- Are new competitors emerging from unexpected quarters?
- Has customer excitement for your offerings disappeared?
- Do employees no longer consider you a top employer?
- Are your best people leaving?
- Is your company undervalued?

Business as usual may only have a finite shelf life.

The need for innovation means that every business should be trying to position its products and services positively against the competition.

Example Technique: One approach to understanding the relative performance of a product is mapping value (e.g. price) against the perceived product performance. To understand this latter dimension, ask current and potential customers to produce a list of the most important characteristics of the service. You can then ask each of them to prioritize those attributes by allocating a number of votes to each particular attribute.

You're looking for several things from these maps as you consider them over time. The first is considering the relative position of your product and service. The second is to zero in on the relative importance and comparison of your key sources of differential advantage compared to the competition.

With this information, you can track how the specific characteristics change over time with new ones appearing and older ones becoming less important. This type of activity (among others) can help you to recognize changes around your company before they become terminal. If you see your relative advantages eroding then you either have to be re-establishing them or finding new sectors in which to compete.

The subtlety here is that this type of monitoring will enable you to track subtle changes but more sudden shifts in what customers want and what they value will be much harder to see coming.

In a similar vein, Donald Keough set out a list of attributes that he suggested lead to business failure. It's like a shopping list of what you should do if you want to destroy your business.

- quit taking risks
- be inflexible
- isolate yourself
- assume infallibility
- play the game close to the foul line
- don't take time to think
- put all your faith in experts and outside consultants
- love your bureaucracy
- send mixed messages
- be afraid of the future.

So what are the big takeaways here?

- **Don't get comfortable.** Probabilities suggest that very few people reading this are in a business that can happily ignore the danger of shifts in their business model.
- **Don't get too busy.** Being face down in the spaghetti of the day-to-day will stop you looking up and seeing what's coming.
- **Pay attention.** Watch for trends and shifts in your competitive advantage and financial results relative to your competition. The rumour goes that one supermarket known for very deep use of data didn't bother doing much face-to-face market research. So they knew everything about what people bought, how often and under what circumstances – but they didn't have much of a clue about changes in attitudes among their customers (if the rumour is true).

Sources

Keough, Donald R., *The Ten Commandments for Business Failure* (Portfolio, New York, 2011)

McGrath, Rita Gunther, *The End of Competitive Advantage: How to Keep Your Strategy Moving as Fast as Your Business* (Harvard Business Review Press, Boston, 2013)

See also

Chapter 15 – Discusses whether the concept of a sustainable or long-term competitive advantage can still exist in many of today's fast-moving markets.

Further reading

Porter, Michael E., *Competitive Advantage* (The Free Press, Cambridge, 2004)

This is the book that really epitomizes thinking about competitive advantage. It is still very relevant but Gunther McGrath's approach is an invaluable addition.

20 MATCHING STRATEGY TO YOUR SITUATION

How to identify the right type of strategy for your organization

Einstein said something along the lines of insanity being someone doing the same thing and expecting a different result. Substitute the words 'right result' into that line and you're on the right track. How can one approach that is fit for the stable environments of the oil and gas industries also be appropriate for the fastest moving technology markets? The simple answer is that the accelerating rate of business failure suggests we can't.

Martin Reeves, Claire Love and Philip Tillmanns work for Boston Consulting Group (BCG) and carried out a survey across 120 companies. The survey included ten different industries and looked at executives' attitudes to strategy.

The researchers' viewpoint is that one size does not fit all in terms of how you think about, create and implement strategy. What they discovered was a widespread recognition of this fact among the executives surveyed but it was allied to a clear failure to act on this knowledge. What the execs actually do is far more classic in terms of strategic thinking than these viewpoints would suggest.

Want some startling results? Those companies that match the style of their strategy to their situation do 4 per cent to 8 per cent better in terms of shareholder returns than those that don't!

Now part of this effect might be that those who recognize the right type of strategy are also smart enough to get the other bits right – e.g. defining the correct strategy, metrics and execution plans to actually deliver it! Nonetheless, the difference in performance cannot and should not be ignored.

The BCG team suggested that the problem for executives is that they don't understand how to go about selecting the best strategy for selecting their strategy.

Now BCG people are pretty smart (I know I've trained some of them, as well as strategy and operational people at Deloitte). The authors simplified this challenging problem into some simple criteria.

First, they want you to think about the 'predictability' of the future environment. If you really can understand market and revenue trends, customer demand, likely competitive actions and other risks, then can I join your industry please as it sounds great! But seriously, some sectors will have high stability and you can have high degrees of confidence about their futures. Others will be far more difficult to predict and some will be almost impossible. That latter shouldn't scare you. It's actually a fun space to work in but it means you have to be constantly vigilant about the world around you and be actively searching ahead for new opportunities, threats, entrants, changes in buyer behaviour etc. – any of which may emerge very quickly.

The second simple criteria the researchers discuss is 'malleability'. That refers to the level of influences that you or competitors can have over the above factors. For example, electricity demand is relatively inelastic. Power companies talk a good game about wanting us to use less electricity but the reality is they want us to keep buying power from them and the long-term decline of usage per person (as we become more environmentally conscious) is pretty slow. They couldn't for myriad reasons start encouraging us to use more and we wouldn't respond as it's nonsensical. That's low malleability in action right there, in a relatively predictable sector.

SO IS THE FIT RIGHT?

If you are going to decide on an approach then it goes without saying that you must absolutely judge the current and foreseen situation correctly in your sector. If you have multiple business units or individual units operating in multiple segments, then you may need to treat each one specifically – providing it with a specific strategy that relates to that part and factors including the malleability and predictability mentioned above.

Here are a few questions that will perhaps help when considering if there is a good match between your strategy and the context.

- Is the strategy leading us to be a 'me too' player or genuinely moving ahead of the market?
- Although sustainable competitive advantage is harder to create, does our strategy lead us to have an advantage at either the company (e.g. cost leadership) or product/service level?
- Can you really identify what the market will do in the next year and beyond? If you were surprised over the past year or so by competitor actions, then chances are you're going to be surprised again. Either the market is becoming less predictable or your ability to identify potential change is below where it needs to be.
- Does the strategy include seeking to understand and potentially embrace uncertainty?
- What sources of bias may have entered the process? Would an independent team form the same conclusion?

The response to some of the questions above should be that if you can't say yes, then why do you think the strategy is correct?

As discussed in a number of chapters, the pace of change in markets is increasing and predictability is to some extent illusory. Hotel chains probably focused on big economic factors such as affordability and spending power of individuals and businesses. They probably eyed each other up carefully to see who was building what capacity where. They would address big events and consider whether their capacity was sufficient. However, they didn't necessarily see Airbnb overtaking the market capitalization of Marriott sometime in 2015 – without a single hotel room to the company's name. The predictability and control they felt was an illusion. A healthy dose of paranoia and a presupposition that your market position will definitely come under attack are better than hoping for the best and getting lost in the day to day of business.

So what are the big takeaways here?

- **One size for strategy does not fit all.** Think honestly about your current situation and get it right. Deluding yourself won't help. Understand your situation correctly and then the correct type of strategy becomes clearer.
- **It's not where you start, it's where you finish.** A company operating in one product area may still need to change over time as the ability to influence a market at the start of its life-cycle may reduce over time – meaning you may have to change the type of strategy you deploy.
- **Question your own biases and presuppositions.** Imagine the company had been taken out by a competitor. How could that happen? What mistakes would you have made? What alternatives could they exploit?
- **Build some alarms into your monitoring of the situation.** If the strategy itself is predicated on certain assumptions, then make these explicit and put in place specific measures to see if these are any longer valid. The lower the predictability, the more you need to be sensitive to changes in the environment.

Source

Reeves, M., Love, C. & Tillmanns, P. (2012), 'Your Strategy Needs a Strategy', *Harvard Business Review*, September 2012

See also

Chapter 14 – Discusses the adaptability required in some businesses that are facing uncertain markets and increasingly effective/intense competition.

Further reading

Rumelt, Richard, *Good Strategy/Bad Strategy* (Profile Books, London, 2012)

21 GENERIC STRATEGY OPTIONS AND WHAT THEY MEAN FOR YOU

Figure out what you want to do and then actually do it

Some concepts stand the test of time. This work dates back to 1993, and is great at helping a company consider how it wants to compete and how this will impact the choices it needs to make. Although similar to Porter's generic strategies for competitive strategy, this approach created by Fred Wiersema and Michael Treacy describes three value disciplines.

The work was based on consulting work and research done for the Index Alliance. It looked at major corporations in the US to identify how companies outperformed their competition. In particular, the authors considered some new entrants that had outstripped their more traditional competitors (e.g. how Nike overtook Adidas).

The work identified three stages in the development of a successful position for the companies.

- The first part was to redefine value for customers.
- The second element was then to be excellent at delivering more of that value for customers.
- The third aspect was how the companies were then able to elevate customer expectations beyond where their competitors could reach at that point.

That might seem quite simplistic. Don't worry, there's more. They also defined three dimensions in which the companies had delivered this value as described below.

Product leadership

This involves delivering differentiated and/or high margin products and so requires strength in skills such as innovation, product development, technology development and branding. The result of this approach will often be the ability to achieve higher margins for a more desirable product.

Apple, BMW, Mercedes-Benz and Sony are companies that show product leadership.

Customer intimacy

Customer intimacy means gaining a deeper understanding of the customer and then delivering tailored products or services to them. This may be an individual product or a bundle of complementary offerings centred around the customer's desires or needs.

Macmillan Cancer Support offers support to those affected by cancer with a very high level of customer intimacy. Its wealth of experience has shaped the care it offers and this includes nursing care in the patient's home but can also range from financial support through to a lift to the hospital. The care provided is different in every case.

McKinsey & Company competes by having its partners work with company CEOs. This ensures the firm understands a company's situation and problems from an insider perspective.

Operational excellence

This is where an organization targets cost leadership in its industry. This is accomplished through the standardization of processes to improve throughput, reduce errors and enable high levels of output at low costs. Economies of scale also help. In manufactured goods, standardizing parts across different products delivers higher volumes of a reduced number of components. The more you produce of the same thing, the lower the unit costs should be.

In service businesses, operational excellence involves streamlining the operation by converting manual processes to automated ones – e.g. capturing customer information online and scanning correspondence.

Organizations need to have a certain capability in each of the disciplines. There is a bare minimum that is needed to compete in the market. The successful companies had moved to a significantly 'stronger' position than their competitors on one (or in exceptional cases two) of the value discipline dimensions.

However, as with Porter's strategies, the danger is in attempting to be all things to all people and try to excel in all three value disciplines. Clearly, the cost-cutting approach of operational efficiency will be difficult to integrate well alongside trying to deliver high levels of customer intimacy.

Wiersema and Treacy also recognize the potential for some companies to master two of the three value disciplines. So who might be good at that now?

Case study: Amazon – Master of two disciplines

Well Amazon is clearly working very hard to optimize the costs of its deliveries. That's the major part of its business according to CEO Jeff Bezos – Amazon delivers! That's what customers expect. That is an example of exceptional operational excellence. In parallel with this, it is also able to offer customer intimacy in the form of tailored recommendations for its customers. Now that is an example of the application of big data in action. The millions of transactions create a wealth of data that Amazon uses to target customers with accessories and further purchases that its data mining suggests will be attractive.

The result is a 'tailored experience' that mimics true customer intimacy while being delivered in a very efficient way. Capturing and mastering customer data is one way that businesses will be able to differentiate themselves on the customer intimacy axis in the future.

Remember, if it includes both business-to-business (B2B) and business-to-consumer (B2C) elements, then it's entirely possible that these parts will work in different ways. For example, in an insurance company, the selling of policies covering directors (Directors and Officers insurance), professional indemnity, etc. is all still mainly done through face to face channels. However, the markets for household and car insurance have now moved almost completely online. The business products retain a strong element of customer intimacy while the 'personal lines' (like car insurance) are all about operational efficiency. The market is cut-throat, margins are slim and no company can afford a direct sales team for these products.

UNDERSTANDING THE STRATEGY CHOICES

The way to apply this thinking is to first of all consider how your company actually competes.

If necessary, you can break this down into different business units or product/service lines. Either way, identify what you think is the primary one of the three value disciplines that your company uses to compete.

The next stage is to consider how well positioned the company is on that particular axis. We'll look at them one by one.

Product leadership

The first thing to say here is that this is mainly about the perception of customers rather than a purely factual assessment. For example, Apple's iPhone was considered the best phone in the world by scores of users when I first started asking them about it. At that point, they were probably correct. Later, the same question would get the same response, although the iPhone's lead had probably been eroded by that stage. In fact, Apple fans were saying the same thing long after the iPhone was clearly no longer the best phone. However, even after the launch of the iPhone 6, owners now freely admit iPhones are no longer the best phones available. That is a scary decline from true product leadership through to something more akin to being a follower – creating larger phones to mimic Samsung and other maker's larger models. Steve Jobs didn't want a 'mini iPad', but again competition forced the company to respond.

Apple is spending US$6 billion on R&D annually (around 3.3 per cent of turnover), so it is obviously keen to catch up and ensure future leadership in some areas.

So back to your company. If product leadership is your primary source of differential advantage, what are you doing to maintain that leadership? What are the projects and programmes that are in place to improve your position? If there aren't any, then the concern must surely be that someone else is going to catch you up sooner or later.

Operational effectiveness

Again, if your company is primarily about operational effectiveness, then what is going on that will help you improve that efficiency? If there is nothing going on then you risk a competitor continuing to improve its position until you find yourself overtaken. So you need to ensure you are actively working to maintain your leadership.

In addition, are you watching alternative means of delivering the same service? That might be an alternative technology or a different channel, but these other mechanisms might enable a company to leapfrog over you.

Customer intimacy

You might think there's a pattern forming here around trying to stay ahead. With customer intimacy, the question is not about what you are doing to increase customer intimacy, as this is easy. Spend more money and dedicate more people to serving your customers. The only problem is the cost associated with that approach.

A better question would be how are you identifying the right level of customer intimacy while reducing costs where possible? That covers the idea that, first, you might need to adjust, either up or down, how close you are to customers. The second part is that you're looking for ways to deliver that intimacy in more efficient ways.

As a final thought, you also need to remember that you might need to excel in two disciplines to succeed. However, whether this is true or not, you absolutely need to ensure that you are strong enough to compete on all three dimensions. If not, you may not remain in the game. For example, great customer service that is way too expensive is a losing proposition.

So what are the big takeaways here?

- **Question your current position... and the ideal future position on all dimensions.** Then ensure you have the projects/programmes in place to get you there.
- **Worry about your competitors creeping up on you.** They will be. Are you staying clear of them and, if not, are you doing enough to re-establish a lead? If you are doing all you can, is it that the source of advantage is becoming less important to your customers. If so, you'll need to find new sources of competitive advantage.
- **The world is changing.** Wherever you are positioned today as a company will continually need to evolve or you simply won't exist.

Source

Treacy, Michael & Wiersema, Fred, *The Discipline of Market Leaders: Choose Your Customers, Narrow Your Focus, Dominate Your Market* (Perseus Books, New York, 1996)

See also

Chapter 12 – Shares some similar thinking on sources of competitive advantage.

22 CREATING ADAPTABILITY TO DEAL WITH A CHANGING ENVIRONMENT

Float like a butterfly...

In our turbulent times, rather than creating rigid targets using rigid approaches, organizations should think differently. Developing a play script that outlines and guides how the business will operate over time may be a better approach.

This chapter will discuss that thought – which you can find reinforced by Richard Rumelt's work on guiding principles and echoed in consulting firms like Deloitte's approach to strategic assignments with its strategic 'design principles'.

In five years studying business across several sectors and in his work on developing strategy, Michael Jacobides, a professor of strategic management at London Business School, nails a serious weakness of traditional approaches.

Many of the classic tools and models were created in times when industries were far more stable. This means that many of the models assume that the boundaries of markets and competition are somehow fixed. They analyse the status quo but are little use in trying to see over the horizon to the very things you need to be considering in great detail – new entrants, competitive shifts, changes in customer preferences, disruptive business models, etc.

The upshot of the characteristics of some models is that you may miss important opportunities/threats or may simply head off down the wrong path.

Jacobides points at game theory and war game simulations as methods that organizations can use to try to model the competitive landscape and future actions/reactions more realistically. However, they are both complex methods and rely on relatively fixed views of the future.

His view is that strategy development requires an organization to fully describe the situation and include the logic involved in strategy choices, storylines, motives and thinking of all the different players in the value chain. That means not just identifying them as occasionally happens with people misapplying Porter's Five Forces model. Instead, you are aiming to understand what your customers, suppliers, competitors, etc. are thinking, how power is shifting between parties, underlying changes, etc.

He refers to this approach as developing a play script. American football players are all expected to memorize their team's play book. It explains how a particular offensive play will work, who runs where, etc. Apart from a few versions where the quarterback has a choice of how to proceed at a particular point (so-called 'read-option plays'), each play is very specific in who does what.

Jacobides's play script is more fluid than this and could be seen as more akin to a treatment for a film or TV programme. He describes the company as the protagonist and lists the actions, activities, decisions and underlying motives of the organization. It also includes the other organizations that are related to the initial organization in some way. He even includes the idea of subplots in the script.

Jacobides says you need to develop two distinct types of play scripts.

Script 1. The Corporate Play Script

As with some of the more interesting modelling approaches, this focuses on how the business generates value and then appropriates it. The subtle distinction between those lines is discussed in more detail in Chapter 18. However, the simple point is that you can generate value but then find that other people within the overall value chain have taken it. Appropriation means getting as much as you can from the value created. Welcome to capitalism 101!

The 'Synergies Subplot' defines how different business units can work together and the way in which the organization will manage these to add value.

The 'Financial Subplot' defines the use of resources and assets to create financial returns for the organization.

Script 2. The Business Play Script

Jacobides views this as more important than the Corporate Play Script. It needs to incorporate:

- Players in the sector, their motivations and roles (e.g. competitors, suppliers, regulators)
- Links and rules that show the connections and relationship between companies and the rules in the organization
- Present and future plots and subplots. This is the storyline of how players in the sector will create value and capture it.

The characteristics of a good play script are defined below.

Imaginative. You want to think beyond your current situation and conventional wisdom. That's non-negotiable.

Outward facing. The play script must be externally focused and consider the relationships with other parties.

Robust. Concentrate on actions that lead to creating and appropriating value – but don't include too many assumptions about the behaviour of other parties in the system.

Plausible. The play script should actually be achievable. If not by you then could someone else achieve it? If not, it fails this test.

Does this all seem a bit esoteric? Is it a bit uncomfortable to move away from nice definite models and charts? I wouldn't disagree. But this approach means you are actually defining your current and future positions while considering the relevant players and steps needed to achieve your goals.

Below, I'll describe the practical steps you can take to produce a play script and you may well feel more comfortable again.

SECURING STRATEGIES BASED ON PLAY SCRIPTS

Jacobides suggests four quick guidelines for when things may be going badly. If one or more of the following are true, you should take care.

1. You have to justify to customers the value you are adding. If this is just true for your company then that's a loss of competitiveness on your part. I'd suggest that if this is true for all competition in the sector, then the underlying business model may be at risk (e.g. you may be moving to a commodity stage or customers may be migrating to other ways to satisfy their needs).
2. When you keep the same relationships to the same players, while those around you are creating new linkages, you should be concerned.
3. You believe customers still value the same things.
4. Players are creating value in adjacent parts of the process (e.g. a supplier to your organization).

To create strategy based around a play script, he defined the following stages with the kind of questions you need to ask. It's elegant and simple. I'd argue that you need to consider some other aspects to completely flesh out this thinking, but that's why there are another 39 chapters in this book! However, I do like this thinking very much.

Define the current sector and play script	Create the new strategy by evolving the play script	Future-proof the play script
Answer these Questions	Answer these Questions	Answer these Questions
Who are the main players (wholesale and retail buyers, consumers, users, competitors, suppliers, regulators, etc.)? **What** are the rules (formal as well as informal) that link between the different actors in the environment? **What** motivates the other actors? **Who** is doing what and why? **What** has changed recently? **What** looks like it may change?	**What** would the best play script be? **Are** there any new, unique parts that could be played by the organization? **How** could you change value creation? **How** could you use the motivations of others to support what you do? **What** parts of the play script can you influence? **Which** new players or roles in the value chain could help your position? **Has** anyone else got a better script?	**How** are customers' needs and preferences changing? **How** do these changes influence who creates and appropriates value? **How** will you remain competitive? **How** can you protect value coming to you rather than being taken by others? **What** responses might there be to playing out your script? **What** relationships can be created to strengthen your position? **What** other resources can help defend your play script?

So what are the big takeaways here?

- **Principles help guide what you should and shouldn't do.** Simple rules and ideas can limit the scope of your strategic options. This is a good thing.
- **Look out for the signs you might be in trouble.** Pose the questions Jacobides suggests but, more broadly, look for changes in the relationships and power between different actors in the environment around you.

- **You can hate the play script concept, but don't hate the game.** Jacobides's thinking is very useful, even if you're not a fan of the play script name. The questions he suggests should be a part of any strategic evaluation and analysis – whether or not you're converting that into a play script or not.

Sources

Jacobides, M. G., 'Strategy Tools for a Shifting Landscape', *Harvard Business Review* , January-February 2010 [https://hbr.org/archive-toc/BR1001]

Rumelt, Richard, *Good Strategy/Bad Strategy* (Profile Books, London, 2012)

See also

Chapter 18 – Discusses how value is generated and appropriated by a company.

Further reading

Lafley, A. G. & Martin, Roger, L., *Playing to Win: How Strategy Really Works* (Harvard Business Review Press, Boston, 2013)

23 LEARNING FROM FAILURE

Feel the fear and do it anyway

In a difficult environment for businesses, failure is an all-too frequent consequence. It exposes individuals to criticism and we normally shy away from it. However, this chapter is going to discuss embracing failure – or at least not avoiding it at all costs.

Many of the chapters in the book talk about rigid thinking and general inflexibility in organizations. Now nobody welcomes the idea of failure but Rita Gunther McGrath has looked at how well organizations learn from failure and how they can embrace it to perform better.

Think about it. If an organization is too frightened to fail, how can it ever experiment and find successful new ways of working. Rita Gunther McGrath acknowledges the interesting reality that lessons can be learned from both deliberate and accidental actions. Failure driven by either can provide useful information.

- Pixar's amazing animated films came from a company that started as a developer of exceptional computer hardware.
- 3M's Post-it® notes benefit from a glue that didn't stick properly.
- The antibiotic properties of penicillin were discovered by accident.

Let's discuss how failures can be helpful.

- **A portfolio of shares or ventures or lots of other things is needed to ensure that at least some succeed.** In sports, they say you miss 100 per cent of the shots you never take, so more shots means more success, we hope. Now clearly there needs to be a balance or you'll spend all your money on potential new things.

- **You can learn what will and won't work.** The founders of Innocent drinks took some time perfecting their smoothie recipes, spent £500 on fruit and set up at a music festival. They placed two bins for empties marked YES and NO with a sign asking if they should quit their jobs and start a smoothie business. All but three bottles went into the YES bin.
- **It shakes things up.** That might be changing the guard at the top of the company or convincing people that a change is needed. In change management, the conventional wisdom is that people will keep doing the same thing, unless the pain of carrying on doing it is greater than the pain of changing. So failure may sometimes be needed to get people or an organization out of a rut.

Gunther McGrath's approach is to prepare for failure and ensure you learn from it. She proposes a number of principles that apply to product/service development, creating a start-up or developing a new technology.

EMBRACING RISK AND FAILURE

Figure out what success and failure look like before you start

In projects this can help to avoid the concept of scope creep but the reverse can also be true. If you don't know what you're aiming for then how do you know if you've succeeded. If there is no consensus then how can you understand what the total upside might be?

Keep questioning assumptions

The concept of confirmation bias suggests we look for information that supports our belief in a situation. To avoid this, Gunther McGrath suggests making all the assumptions explicit at the start so they are out in the open. Then you keep going back to them and replace them with facts as you proceed. Facts may support or disprove an assumption but either way you want the quality of information to be improving over time.

It's Barbara Minto's Pyramid Principle in action. Her approach suggests developing a hypothesis for a situation. It doesn't need to be true today. Instead, you go about defining all the things that have to be true for the hypothesis to be true. By breaking these down into more and more detailed supporting points, you end up with a complete list of what must be true. Beyond this, the Pyramid Principle approach defines the work you need to do to test each aspect that supports the hypothesis.

You're looking for mutually exclusive and collectively exhaustive points. That means there is no overlap between different parts of the breakdown and you're looking to cover all the bases.

Limit uncertainty

In a variant of thought about the Ansoff Matrix choices for increasing revenues beyond the existing areas (that will be discussed in Chapter 27), Gunther McGrath suggests taking new products to your existing markets or existing products to new markets.

She, sensibly, is less convinced about the diversification route of products that are new to the firm being delivered to new markets.

Celebrate intelligent failure

As with encouraging children, rewarding the effort can be as important as celebrating success. If failure is always criticized openly in the company culture, don't be surprised if the organization as a whole appears risk averse.

There's a further aspect to this. If you have a culture where the messenger is shot, you're risking people delaying admissions about things going wrong. The approaches Gunther McGrath is talking about thrive on openness and honesty as early on as possible in the process. You might not like bad news but work to hear it as early as possible before the problem becomes a crisis.

Manage the downside risk

Find ways to get your first indication of success cheaply. A great question in managing risks is to ask what the first indication would be that something is going wrong. If you can define that then you have your early warning system in place. With these projects you want to identify early signs that it is going to fail. That way you minimize wastage of resources and time.

Fail fast

If you think about it, then failing fast makes a lot of sense. It allows you to redirect resources elsewhere as well as integrating the learning quickly. You can start an alternative course of action if that makes sense and reapply resources to another activity.

R. G. Cooper's 'Stage-Gate®' approach is an example of trying to minimize the poor use of resources on projects. It uses criteria at each 'gate' to help the organization decide if the project can proceed to the next stage of work. In this way, progress is a series of controlled steps where you only enter the next, larger investment of time, money and resources if the project seems favourable. If the criteria are well selected and the process followed correctly, you would hope bad projects will be halted by it.

Share learning

Obvious really, but you need to think about how you capture learning and share it. What do they say? Those who ignore the lessons of history are forced to relive them. The same thing applies to organizations.

So what are the big takeaways here?

- **Design work to identify failure early.** Think about ways in which you can take risks but with built-in indicators that you're going to fail that will become evident early on.
- **Fail fast – fail often.** Move on from looking to reconfirm your current thinking. Instead, exploring outside of the corporate comfort zone can help you understand what will and won't work.
- **Expose your assumptions.** If you can explore and bring your assumptions to the surface, you can go about questioning them one by one. Not only can you check out the chain of assumptions that lead to a particular conclusion, but you can also examine each one to consider its validity. Beyond that

you can play with an assumption and change it. What would happen if this (assumption) wasn't true? What other options are possible? How did we come to this assumption?

Source

Amit, R. & Zott, C. (2012), 'Creating Value Through Business Model Innovation', *MIT Sloan Management Review*, spring 2012

See also

Chapters 24, 25 and 26 – Provide different perspectives on how to work with your business model.

Further reading

Cooper, Robert G., *Winning at New Products: Creating Value Through Innovation* (Basic Books, New York, 2011)

Minto, Barbara, *The Pyramid Principle: Logic in Writing and Thinking* (FT/Prentice Hall, Harlow, 2009)

24 CREATING NEW BUSINESS MODELS

How to build innovative business models

Raphael Amit and Christoph Zott, both professors of entrepreneurship, have done extensive work on relating business model innovation to the creation of value in businesses.

They quote an Economist Intelligence Unit survey that showed that 54 per cent of managers prefer the idea of a new business model over new products/services. This is perhaps indicative of how many consider their current business model to be facing difficulties. A similar study by IBM indicated that companies who had performed well over the previous five years, with growth in operating margins above that of competitors, were twice as likely to emphasize business model innovation over product/process innovation.

They quote a CEO who provides an insight into the underlying logic in these findings. Companies have been working hard to optimize operations and processes as well as cut costs. There is only so much they can do in these areas and so innovation in new areas is important as an alternative source of differentiation.

Amit and Zott looked at 59 ebusiness companies in the US and Europe that had floated via an IPO. Each company was then investigated across 50 questions to produce a working theory about how value is created in these businesses. Beyond this, they then looked at 190 entrepreneurial companies to test their theories about how value is created by their business models. There's more about what they did but the bottom line is that this was thorough and well thought through research.

One interesting focus of their findings is that the business model innovation is discussed in the context of established businesses, not start-ups. This makes it relevant to many more businesses.

Business model innovation provides the chance to exploit new opportunities in your existing market or create a new market.

They suggest innovation could come from a number of different areas:

Content

This refers to the activities in the business and might, for example, involve integration of part of the overall value chain. For example, Chinese mobile handset manufacturers have moved from supplying to well-known companies to creating their own brands, in competition with their own customers.

Structure

This is about how activities in the business can be connected in innovative ways. There are many examples of so called 'disintermediation', where a business that sits between suppliers and customers is leapfrogged. This is so frequent as to be a classic concern for any business that finds itself in that middle ground. As an example, car and home insurance in the UK is now mainly done online, having almost completely displaced broking firms located on the high street.

Governance

This refers to changes in the parties involved in delivery of any part of the business. Car companies have been particularly innovative in this area, recognizing that the assembly of components does not have to be done by them. They have put in place contracts where suppliers deliver completed sub-assemblies (e.g. a rear axle) rather than just parts.

WHAT TO LOOK FOR IN A NEW BUSINESS MODEL

The authors defined four drivers that you should be looking for and considering when exploring alternative business models.

- **Novelty** – Describes the level of innovation in the business model. Airbnb is a highly innovative and novel business model – connecting people wanting accommodation directly with property owners who can provide a place to stay. Airbnb doesn't need to own a single hotel room to compete with hotels that have spent years building up a property portfolio.
- **Lock-in** – Relates to how the business model creates barriers to switching away from the company. These might be costs that customers must meet to go elsewhere (e.g. if you want to play Xbox games but currently have a PS4, your only option would be to buy a second expensive console). These barriers might also be incentive based. Hotels.com provides discounted rooms as a reward for every ten nights you book with the company. If you book elsewhere, you don't get this benefit.
- **Complementarities** – The authors cite the relationship between eBay and PayPal in creating an easy process for buying from the online shopping portal. Interestingly, eBay announced that it would be floating off PayPal during 2014 as the close association with eBay is hampering PayPal's ability to compete with global payment companies in a world filling with innovative competitors like TransferWise (low cost international transfers) and Apple Pay (near field payment in stores using your iPhone).
- **Efficiency** – Refers to the ability to save costs throughout the full set of business activities.

Amit and Zott provide six questions to help tease out potential sources of innovation within an organization's business model.

1. What needs could be met through the new business model? I'd stress that these should primarily relate to things in the mind of the customer but not exclusively. If customers perceive something has value then that is very powerful but other aspects of how the business delivers can also be very important – even though the

specific innovation is essentially invisible to customers. The hope is that the effect of it will be experienced by them.

2. What activities would need to be in place to satisfy the needs identified in 1? This would be business model content innovation.
3. Could these activities be linked together in an innovative way – business model structure innovation?
4. Who should perform each of the activities in the business model – governance innovation?
5. Where different parties are performing the activities, how is value created for each of them?
6. What revenue model would best be aligned with the business model to capture the most value?

In structuring a process to answer these, you need to ensure the team has enough representation from across the business (and potentially beyond) to find the best model at that point.

So what are the big takeaways here?

- **Business model innovation is key.** Even if you don't feel the need to change the model at the time, going through this process may help identify better models or a weakening of the existing one.
- **Aim to generate lots of ideas, then manage them down to the best ones.** This process will benefit from rigorous, careful management. At some points you need creative thinking to generate new ideas and this should not be suppressed by being overly critical. Later on, these ideas will need to be carefully evaluated and challenged. Keep telling people where you are in the process to get the best from it and ensure they are in the right mode. Otherwise you risk stifling every idea before you've had a good chance to consider it.
- **Revolution not evolution.** Okay that's a slight exaggeration, but small incremental changes to products and services are business-as-usual stuff. This process seeks to look further into the future and be more creative.

Source

Amit, R. & Zott, C. (2012), 'Creating Value Through Business Model Innovation', *MIT Sloan Management Review*, spring 2012

See also

Chapters 25 and 26 – Extend the thinking about business model innovation, considering how to identify new business models and then how to add risk to your approach, in the hope of moving from 'me too' approaches to more revolutionary ones.

Further reading

Cooper's thinking on new product development and innovation is widely used and an excellent way to focus finite resources in the right areas and ensure only the right projects proceed towards product/service launch.

Cooper, Robert G., *Winning at New Products: Creating Value Through Innovation* (Basic Books, New York, 2011)

25

HOW TO IDENTIFY NEW BUSINESS MODELS

A structured approach to creating options for your business model

Joseph Sinfield and his colleagues have followed a similar path to Amit and Zott's work, described in Chapter 24.

They suggest that organizations look for growth through three generic options:

- Investment into product/service development to improve what they offer and/or find new products.
- Work hard to understand customer motivations and perceptions – using these to better meet current and potential customer needs.
- Develop strategies to grow through merger and acquisition type activities or movement into other markets.

All three are time and resource hungry.

Sinfield et al suggest the 'fourth way' is through business model experimentation.

As described in Chapter 24, a structured approach can be incredibly useful in exploring optional ways to discovering innovative new business models and approaches to creating value for the business. The authors cite work by Malone et al at MIT Sloan, which looks at why some business models work better than others. Given the importance in maintaining or enhancing competitive positions, the authors underline that getting good at producing business model innovation is a vital competency for an organization.

Their review of other leading-edge thinking suggests 40 different potential components in a business model. However, they use a simple set of fundamental questions that seem to build on thinking from people like Peter Drucker.

- Who is the target customer?
- What is the need being met for them?
- What will the product/service be?
- How does the customer get access to the product/service?
- What is our role in fulfilling the need within the overall value chain?
- How will we make money while doing this?

Where necessary, each of these questions can be decomposed into more detail to try to generate more relevant options. So, for example, the customer question could be deepened with further questions such as:

- Will we serve businesses or consumers?
- Which customers will we serve within that category – high end, value conscious, etc.?
- Which geographies will we cover?
- This can help generate more detailed input for the matrix of different options.
- In terms of what is sold, the authors suggest a useful narrowing set of questions as follows.

Product	OR	Service
Custom	OR	Off-the-shelf
Tangible	OR	Intangible
Generic	OR	Branded
Consumable	OR	Durable

BUILDING A NEW BUSINESS MODEL

The first part of using this thinking is to create a template for the different questions. In each category, a number of options can then be defined as shown in the following table.

Who is target customer?	What need is being filled?	What is the product/ service?	How will the customer access the product/ service?	Where will the company sit in the Value Chain?	How will we make money?
Group 1	Need 1	Offering 1	Channel 1	Role 1	Approach 1
Group 2	Need 2	Offering 2	Channel 2	Role 2	Approach 2
Group 3	Need 3	Offering 3	Channel 3	Role 3	Approach 3

Figure 25.1 A business model template

The next stage is then to consider different combinations across the categories. Sinfield and his colleagues suggest you treat these options like switches as you explore different combinations. One such path is shown in the following diagram.

Who is the target customer?	What need is being filled?	What is the product/ service?	How will the customer access the product/ service?	Where will the company sit in the value chain?	How will we make money?
Group 1	Need 1	Offering 1	Channel 1	Role 1	Approach 1
Group 2	Need 2	Offering 2	Channel 2	Role 2	Approach 2
Group 3	Need 3	Offering 3	Channel 3	Role 3	Approach 3

Figure 25.2 Exploring business model combinations

In a given market/industry, even changing one variable can result in a dramatically different business model. Let's use the telecoms industry as an example. I've moved the Product/Service part to the end to show the differences created by changing that variable.

Who is target customer?	What need is being filled?	How will the customer access the product/ service?	Where will the company sit in the Value Chain?	How will we make money?	What is the product/ service?	Examples
Business callers	Voice → Shops	Role 1	Sell minutes →	VOIP	Skype
Residential– light users	Conferencing	Own store	Service Provider	Subscription bundle	Traditional phone line	AT&T, BT
Residential – international callers	Video	Online	Role 3	–	Mobile	Sprint, Orange, Vodafone

Figure 25.3 A business model example: international phone calls

The simple change produces three different types of business with very different players and pricing. Mobile players will tend to charge high prices per minute for international calls. Skype and other VOIP players will charge very low prices. The typical incumbent operators will be somewhere in between depending on how much they want to compete with the low-cost providers.

One effect in doing this work is that some choices will effectively render other choices obsolete. You won't sell a luxury car online. You can't attract customers in the 'innovator' category if your product is a 'me too'.

The choices can be limited further in a way that isn't artificial or arbitrary, by linking the choices to the overall scope and direction set out in the strategy. If there are some aspects of that which are non-negotiable, then that should be reflected in the selection of options.

For example, if the customer group is defined and not open to discussion, there is no point defining any alternatives in that category in the template. This can be refined with options in each category defined as to whether they are Desirable, Discussable or Unthinkable (as shown in the table below).

	Who is target customer?	What need is being filled?	What is the product/ service?	How will the customer access the product/ service?	Where will the company sit in the Value Chain?	How will we make money?
DESIRABLE	Group 1	Need 1	Offering 1	Channel 1	Role 1	Approach 1
	Group 2			Channel 2	Role 2	
					Role 3	Approach 2
DESIRABLE	Group 3	Need 2				
UNTHINKABLE	Group 4	Need 3	Offering 2	Channel 3		Approach 3
			Offering 3			

Figure 25.4 Refining choices across the business model

So what are the big takeaways here?

- **Create and destroy.** This type of experimentation is valuable as it develops options for you and should be encouraged. You will understand better where your company can and should compete. You will also be able to compare business models to identify which delivers the most value to the business as well as prioritizing the use of scarce resources. After creating options, you are then destroying bad options that don't work for you or that are a bad fit.
- **Tailor the options to your situation.** Which options are open to you in the different categories and which are not. You'll reduce the complexity of what you are considering while also making the exercise more relevant.
- **This approach is not the total solution.** Although it's very valuable as a standalone model, overlapping this approach with other techniques for driving business model innovation will provide the best results.

Source

Sinfield, J. V., Calder, E., McConnell, B. & Colson, S., 'How to identify new business models', *MIT Sloan Management Review*, winter 2012

See also

Chapter 24 – Identifies some ways to innovate around a business model.

Chapter 26 – Introduces the concept of a controlled approach to adding risk to the model. This is important in the context of Chapter 23 , which underlines how important it can be to learn from failure.

MANAGING RISK IN YOUR BUSINESS MODEL

Hope for the best, but plan for the worst

Karan Girotra is a professor of technology and operations management at INSEAD and works alongside Serguei Netessine, professor of global technology and innovation. Together they have looked into the development of improved business models.

They identify the three elements that comprise most business model innovation thinking as:

- Revenues – overall market size, customer numbers, pricing
- Costs – direct costs (cost of sales/cost of goods sold), overheads, capital expenditures, ability to get down the cost reduction curve (economies of scale)
- Resource velocity – describing how quickly different parts of the business create value. What is meant by that is process times, output, stock turn and other measures of revenues compared to the assets used by the business to create them. Improving these is part of classic operational management.

So that's the part that is relatively well understood. The bit that Girotra and Netessine highlight as being neglected is the way that risk can affect these value drivers. Think about it for a second. Most business model innovation aims to produce the best 'upside' case – perhaps a new market area with other changes to support some shiny new revenues. Assuming that the model will simply achieve the expected results is sloppy thinking. It might, but if you don't consider the ways in which it might fail, then you're neglecting things. Whoever said, 'Hope for the best, but plan for the worst', was right. Listen to them – they're making sense!

The authors also quote the economist Robert Merton and the central tenet of their work has echoes of his 2005 article in the *Harvard Business Review*, entitled 'You have more capital than you think'.

He goes beyond considering a company's comparative advantages in simply exploiting opportunities. He adds in thinking about risks. Some companies will have comparative advantages in their abilities to handle or withstand risk.

Now you can think about managing risk in a number of ways. When I'm working on business models, I frequently take a quick look at sensitivities such as lower-than-expected sales, or a growth curve that occurs 6 or 12 months later than expected. Although not as revealing as techniques such as real option techniques, the results are still useful in understanding the impact of delays, slow take-ups, lower sales than expected, etc.

These are classic and rather simple approaches to risk management. However, the authors explain that you need to consider the impact of risk on the overall business model and also how it will be managed or mitigated.

Once you start thinking about risk in the business model, you can begin to think about ways in which the model could be modified to limit or even eliminate some of those risks.

The authors suggest that shaking down a potential business model, or improving an existing one, requires you to look across the value chain to identify the risks.

The next step is to then how these risks can be managed. You can:

- Reduce them
- Shift them to other people
- Take them on yourself – increase the risk! Okay that sounds odd but what it's saying is consider taking on more risk to then maybe discover an innovative business model.

I'll go into more detail on how to think about applying these options in the application section that follows.

HOW TO REDUCE YOUR RISK

So let's look at some of the practical steps that can be taken to mitigate/eliminate the risks that have been identified.

The authors outlined a few approaches.

Speeding up the production process

Girotra and Netessine talk about how Zara reduced the full design cycle for clothes through to production down from 18 months to as little as 2 weeks. That means you can respond to changes in fashion almost instantly and reduce the risk of having to write off stock that appears in the stores after fashion has moved on – or a failure to have enough stock of an item that takes off.

The improved cycle times make Zara more nimble, and although it might be trading off some economies of scale in return, the results seem to justify the approach.

Google uses a pre-signup process for its broadband service, to mitigate the risk that demand in an area they roll out to will be insufficient. By only going to areas of confirmed demand, it makes sure it will make a return on its investments in an area.

Change your contracts

An alternative approach to managing risks is to change the contractual relationship with other people involved in the value chain. That might be employees, suppliers or even your customers.

Zero-hour contracts may not be popular with employees but they do allow a company to flex its workforce on a daily basis without the downsides (to the business) of having to pay those employees regardless of the workload and of them accruing employment rights.

Small suppliers are getting Amazon to fulfil their orders as it means they are present in Amazon's marketplace and can rely on the delivery power of the enormous firm. That's two risks managed but traded off against the likely higher delivery costs they need to pay Amazon – compared to the amount it would cost to manage delivery themselves.

Improve the data you use

As an example of this, let's take the above example on a step further, the deliveries that Amazon do for smaller suppliers also works for them. By managing these deliveries, Amazon effectively has a sales laboratory where it can see what sells and what doesn't. The data on its own sales is supplemented by the suppliers' sales data but without the need to invest in the vast range of products it fulfils for others. However, if Amazon spots high-selling items through its own channels, it can add them to its own list of items. It learns from other people's successes and failures.

Another example is Walkers crisps, which uses competitions to both provide publicity and interactions with its clients. However, some of the competitions also have a simpler purpose. They allow customers to propose new flavours, which are then market-tested over a period of time. The process provides the company with a stream of publicity opportunities and product ideas created and tested by customers.

Shift the risks

The third option section is about increasing risk exposure. That seems counterintuitive until we frame it a different way. In what ways can the company take on risk to help create an innovative new business model? So you're only doing this if you get something out of it. Otherwise, it would be a crazy approach.

So the authors suggest that this is often a shifting of risk from the customer/consumer back onto a supplier. For example, the probability of a washing machine breaking down is relatively low and, although the cost of a repair may be as much as the machine cost originally, the expected cost of repairs over a few years would be quite low. If we had 1,000 washing machines it might average out at a certain sum. Now because we consumers are risk averse, we don't necessarily think about the probable cost to us.

Instead we think about whether we can afford the worst case. Retailers have spotted this opportunity and sell quite expensive extended warranties that are not a rational purchase for their customers. The warranty may be several times more than the customer is likely to pay on repairs, but they are protecting themselves against a major breakdown. The retailer takes on the risk and creates a secondary, high margin source of revenue for themselves.

So what are the big takeaways here?

- **Avoiding risk is not acceptable.** Playing safe will lead you to a 'me too' position that will be short of competitive advantage and which will probably limit the survival of the organization in the long term. So if you need to take risks, and you do, then how well you can do this will also be a potential source of advantage. Being mindlessly reckless will probably end badly. Being able to judge the fine balance between that recklessness and smart gambles will be an important differentiator.
- **Manage the risks aggressively.** The better you can shift them onto others, mitigate them, minimize them or avoid them, the better you will do.
- **Prepare to rip up the rule book.** Conventional wisdom says go for economies of scale. Reduce your costs with big runs of the same thing. That can make a lot of sense. However, that might lead to piles of dead stock in a market built around public tastes. You can't sell the huge stock if tastes change on you quickly. There's no recommendation on which to do – it's about recognizing that there are alternatives to consider.

Sources

Girotra, K. & Netessine, S., 'How to Build Risk into Your Business Model', *Harvard Business Review*, May 2011

Netessine, S., 'Why Large Companies Struggle With Business Model Innovation', *The Renaissance Innovator*, 28 September 2013 (http://renaissanceinnovator.com/2013/09/28/why-large-companies-struggle-with-business-model-innovation)

See also

Chapter 23 – Provides a useful perspective on failure as an important learning tool.

Further reading

Merton. R. C., 'You Have More Capital Than You Think', *Harvard Business Review*, November 2005 (https://hbr. org/2005/11/you-have-more-capital-than-you-think/ar/1)

27 SUSTAINABILITY, FEASIBILITY AND ACCEPTABILITY (SFA ANALYSIS)

Does a potential strategy fit?

A really elegant way of considering strategic options was proposed by Johnson and Scholes.

It seems simple in that it considers a strategy against just three criteria – sustainability, feasibility and acceptability. However, although there are only three, each is considered in an appropriate level of detail and the thinking behind this model is very useful.

Before looking at them in more depth, it's important to understand the information that will be available to you at this point.

The organization's situation should have been reviewed. I'd suggest that this would involve some if not all of the following 'classic' elements.

Understanding the current strategic situation

External factors	Internal factors
Pest analysis	TOWS Analysis (SWOT but in a different order)
Porter's Five Forces	McKinsey 7-S (or similar assessment of internal capabilities)

Leading to...

Strategic options
Porter's Value Chain
Ansoff Matrix
Product Proposition
Porter's Competitive Positions
Wiersema's Three Types of Organizational Focus
Business Model Innovation

Now do everything else you've read in the other 39 chapters in the book and you're ready. Okay that's a bit much but the outcome of all this thinking should be some potential strategic scenarios and a weight of information backing those up. Both are needed to feed into the SFA analysis.

Okay, so it's time to look at the three criteria in more detail.

Sustainability

The S in SFA stands for sustainability. You're looking at whether a strategic option does a number of important things. Does it

- respond to issues identified during the strategic analysis?
- provide appropriate economies of scale and cost position?
- adequately exploit any opportunities available to the company?
- adequately protect against any perceived threats?
- deliver the right level of ambition?
- respond to changes in the external or competitive landscapes?

Feasibility

This revolves around whether the finite set of resources available to the organization can be deployed in a way that will achieve the desired objectives.

In assessing this, the work will revolve more around the detailed assessments you would see in a business case. That means spreadsheets that consider the interrelationships between revenues and costs. That involves building up a model that considers the different markets under consideration, customer numbers over time, the evolution of revenues, etc., and balances these against the capital expenditure and operating expenses that will be needed to support the revenues.

The funding assumptions and interactions between different elements for the operation will be exposed during this exercise. If more working capital is needed then you may need to increase debt, which will increase interest charges, etc. At some point in this iterative exercise, it may become clear that the financial position may not be appropriate for external sources of funding such as banks. If that's the case then you need to iterate more until you get an acceptable set of assumptions and consequent financial results – or are sure that there is no feasible approach.

Acceptability

This final step is to use the information gained in the first two steps, as well as that wealth of background data delivered prior to this analysis, to consider if the strategic option will deliver in line with shareholders' expectations. Is the trade-off between risk and return acceptable? This will be an exercise in balancing that compromise between higher risk, higher return options and safer but less financially rewarding options.

APPLYING SFA THINKING

Thinking about sustainability

In order to compare options against the different performance for sustainability, an approach is to use a weighted factor analysis. In this approach, you would identify the different relevant criteria relating to sustainability. These criteria would then be weighted so that each has an importance percentage where the total across all the criteria is 100 per cent.

For each scenario you then assess a score against each criterion. The score in each category is then multiplied by the weighting (the percentage you defined) and all of these products (category score times weighting) are totalled. This gives an overall score for each scenario.

This is simply one approach to ranking the scenarios against the sustainability criteria.

Thinking about feasibility

There are some aspects of feasibility that are not related to numbers but that are also important. For example, are the changes that would be needed to deliver the strategy going to be possible in the time frames envisaged? An option might require substantial change to the skills or roles/responsibilities within the organization. How would that be done and how much would it cost? What is the likely response of unions to the changes? Will politicians be talking about such changes? What will it all do to your reputation (and does that matter)?

If new skills are needed to execute one or more of the options, then are there any issues about the availability of these skills? Will you need to retrain people internally or get workers to join you from competitors?

In other words, can you realistically change the organization and the correct hard (structure, financially related) and soft (people related) variables? Can you do it fast enough?

Another thing to consider is whether there are enough customers. Will those customers be sufficiently attracted by your offering to come to you in the numbers required? Have you got the sales and back office staff to support these sales in the way you would like? What are the likely competitive responses and how might that change things for you?

There is nothing worse than an approach that assumes 'everything goes right'. Sustainability is about considering a realistic range of outcomes – not living in cloud cuckoo land.

How it might go wrong – and avoiding that possibility

However, it's not quite that simple in that you also need to be ensuring that the options are measured in the right way so that relatively safe strategic options are not selected where they do not support the medium-term survival of the company.

So how can the wrong strategy still be selected when all this work has been done? Actually, the veneer of analysis and numbers can hide a multitude of sins. In an extreme case, imagine if a strategic option that does not answer fundamental problems or threats has somehow remained on the table. The SFA analysis may not actually try to measure the area where the fatal problem lies. Or it may be one of a number of different criteria. Although the 'bad' strategy may score 0 for this category in the weighted factor analysis, it may still come out top of the available options because of its other scores.

The solution is to insert a simple filter in your evaluations. If there are any 'no-go' options or approaches that are plainly unacceptable, filter them out before you get to the SFA stage.

So what are the big takeaways here?

- **Weed out stupid strategies.** Kill any inappropriate strategic options early and clearly in the process. Otherwise you risk the maths of any analysis somehow selecting this type of 'wrong' answer.
- **Think clearly.** Are we applying this analysis fairly and correctly? Are we letting biases sway our opinion?
- **SFA is for evaluation – not strategy creation.** SFA analysis won't help you develop a great strategy if it wasn't in the mix at the start of this exercise. But if it is there somewhere, SFA is a good tool to help eliminate weaker strategies and hopefully help pick the right one.

Source

Johnson, Gerry, Scholes, Kevan & Whittington, Richard, *Exploring Corporate Strategy* (FT/Prentice Hall, Harlow, 2007)

See also

This is a tool for reviewing what you've created as a potential strategy. To that extent, every other chapter feeds into this one.

Further reading

Lafley, A.G. & Martin, Roger L., *Playing to Win: How Strategy Really Works* (Harvard Business Review Press, Boston, 2013)

Porter, Michael E., *Competitive Strategy: Techniques for Analyzing Industries and Competitors* (The Free Press, New York, 2004)

28 BOLD RETREAT

Sometimes reverse is the right direction

Much of strategic language comes from military strategy and the analysis of wisdom found in Sun Tzu's book *The Art of War* and Carl von Clausewitz's *On War*. We talk of defence, retrenching, flanking attacks and other terms straight from the battlefield.

One of Adner and Snow's contributions to strategic thinking discusses a position that would be humiliating in military circles – a retreat!

The foundation of their thinking is that more established technology companies, when faced with a new technology, will either try to fight it head on or will try to transition to it over time. To continue the military metaphor … for some technology battles that would be the older technology trying to charge machine guns. It's a losing battle and one that's likely to hurt.

Instead of trying to copy or take on the new entrant, Adner and Snow instead suggest a retreat might sometimes be in order. However, they aren't talking about a slow slinking off into a corner. They advocate a bold retreat where the company either retrenches to a niche within its traditional market (if one exists) or a move to a new market where the old technology is superior to competitive offerings. You might argue that the latter is so bold that it probably shouldn't be termed a retreat and I would agree. However, the concept is more important than the label!

The researchers talk about this being a retreat, which implies that you are returning to a position you have previously occupied. However, they point out that either type of retreat will require significant organizational change to properly execute.

Adner and Snow explain that strategic options can often be framed as moves forward for the business and these variations of retreats can be overlooked. However, they add that it can be hard for managers to bring themselves to consider a retreat when 'good management' is framed around growth. The individual's ego may simply get in the way.

Retrenching to a niche

The problem with competition from a new technology is that it changes the value proposition for customers. The new and the old will not overlap but the company should consider if the new technology has left any customer needs unmet. It's not just that there are some areas that are not addressed by the new technology; there are also some lessons that can be drawn when you consider the dominating attributes of the new technology.

The example they cite is about how quartz watch technology provided superior accuracy to traditional, mechanical watches. However, it was possible once quartz watches appeared to recognize that some customers preferred a watch with a mechanical movement. That was impossible to identify before the quartz watch provided an option.

Companies that identified this customer preference in the watch market started to display the inner workings of their watches with transparent windows that show off the previously hidden complexity of these timepieces.

This subset of the market was a niche that some of the traditional watchmakers could continue to exploit.

Relocation to a new market

This is consistent with the Ansoff Matrix where you're either going to fix new problems for your current customers or the same problems for new customers.

A good question is if these markets existed before, why weren't they adequately served?

The answer may be, if the market truly exists, that when things were going well for the company, this new market was relatively unattractive and/or might have been considered a distraction from the primary markets. However, once the new technology appears and threatens the primary market, the new market may appear more attractive than it had previously. A lifeboat looks great if your ship is sinking. It probably didn't carry much appeal beforehand.

WORKING OUT IF YOU SHOULD RETREAT

Adner and Snow suggest an eight-step process to consider whether retrenching is the right option.

1. What does the new technology ignore in terms of value creation – e.g. performance, how it's delivered, aspects of quality, add-ons, etc.?
2. Which customers care about these attributes that are not fully addressed by the new technology?
3. If the company focused on those attributes, how else could the value proposition be enhanced for the group of susceptible customers?
4. If the company moves to the niche and is able to dominate it, is there enough there to make it worthwhile (revenues, margins, etc.)?
5. To make this move, what changes would be needed within the organization (thinking about processes, metrics, roles and responsibilities, personal attributes, systems, etc.)?
6. What will the competition be like in the niche?
7. If we move to the niche then does the current set of suppliers and partners support this new positioning adequately?
8. Compared to other strategic choices, how attractive is this option?

In a similar way, the researchers suggest questions to help consider if a new market will be attractive.

1. If the old technology was available at no cost, who would want it and what might they do with it?
2. Are there reasons why people who might use the old technology are not currently using it? (E.g. price, availability, specifications, quality.)

3. What is the alternative technology these users are using instead and why? What are they paying for the alternative?
4. What changes would be needed to the company's own technology to serve the customers identified at that same price point (or better)?
5. How much more value would the customers identified above receive from using the company's technology? In other words, what's it worth to them? This has to be balanced against the costs and difficulty of serving these customers, the uniqueness and advantage of the offer and also the barrier to the current technology they are replacing.
6. Considering the other strategic alternatives, is entering this new market the right option for the company?

Going through with these types of strategies is going to have serious implications for the company.

The company needs to be refocused and maybe rebuilt

You're going to have to not just change the market but also alter channels, sales teams, skills, structure and potentially increase parts of the business while shrinking others. The retrenching or new market(s) are more often going to lead to a reduction in revenues and, potentially, margins. The business is going to have to match itself to this more challenging reality.

Partners and suppliers may also need to change and you may find that some no longer wish to work with you. Cosy relationships and attractive terms may no longer be available and this may affect assumptions about the new business case.

As a final point, consider having to convince a group of shareholders about the wisdom of this bold and exciting move when all they are going to focus on, at least initially, is the fact that revenues are going down and the company is less stable than it was. It's a rare and brave CEO that would enjoy such a discussion.

In change management, the phrase 'the pain of staying where you are has to be greater than the pain of the change, otherwise people won't change'. It's completely true in this case. The case that the business cannot remain where it is needs to be made before the new markets or retrenched position are put forward.

So what are the big takeaways here?

- **Always consider retreat options.** That means before you even develop a single cunning scenario, you have the 'do nothing', steady as one generic approach that you must always consider. The retreat option is another generic choice that you must always have in play – even if it is not as prominent in your thinking. Now in both cases, the scenarios need to be fleshed out to consider the implications but it does mean that you could and should start with two strategic options on the table before you have even really started the strategy process.
- **'Burn the platform'.** Make sure people understand why the 'old way' is no longer valid and alternatives must be found. Otherwise, they won't necessarily commit to finding and adopting the new way of doing business.
- **You may be retreating to a place you've never been.** Retreat sounds easy as it implies you're going back to a position the company held previously. That's not the case. The upheaval and extent of change can easily be as significant as in strategies based around growth, M&A (mergers and acquisitions) or other good news stories for the business. Change is always hard.

Source

Adner, R. & Snow, D. C., 'Bold retreat: a new strategy for old technologies', *Harvard Business Review*, March 2010

See also

The next few chapters will consider more aggressive alternatives that complement this chapter.

Further reading

You can read more about the Ansoff Matrix and other models in marketing, strategy and portfolio management in:

Jones, Richard A. D., *One Day MBA: Skills For Succeeding in Business Today* (Winmark/ICSA, London, 2012)

29 STRATEGY – ART OR SCIENCE

How concentrating on data and what is true today, can make you miss what will be important tomorrow

That might sound a strange assertion since much of what is discussed in terms of strategy involves detailed numerical analyses and production of huge Excel spreadsheets to try to model the financial results of a complex set of assumptions.

In spite of the volume of data and numbers crunched, Lafley et al suggest that most strategic planning is actually not rigorous and is unscientific.

They put forward a structured process based on Procter and Gamble's approach and its success with reinvigorating the skin care product Olay.

The main difference to traditional approaches was to move from asking:

'What is the right answer?'
to
'What are the right questions?'

The group believed that typical strategic planning often gets drawn into focusing on issues such as a product or service losing margin or a market in decline. The problem is that the data gathering and analysis then tends to focus around this issue rather than looking at potential solutions or even more revolutionary strategic moves.

To avoid this, they favour a possibilities-based approach that reminds me strongly of Barbara Minto's work in *The Pyramid Principle* (another must-read). If you've read her work (or my description in Chapter 23), you'll remember Minto's approach is about defining hypotheses to then create a structured approach to work that will confirm or refute the hypothesis. It does this by considering all the things that have to be true for the hypothesis to be correct. Variations of this approach are enshrined in consulting companies' work. For example, this is part of what I teach to operational consultants in a big four consulting firm.

Lafley and the team suggest formulating two opposing hypotheses that are mutually exclusive. I'd maybe layer on the idea from Pyramid-type thinking that would say the hypotheses must be sufficiently exhaustive and mutually exclusive. In other words, they need to be sufficiently detailed to fully capture the choice they relate to but not overlap.

Once such a choice can be defined, the strategy team is now going to be focused on what comes next.

Their work considers P&G's choice in the skin care market between revamping and repositioning its Oil of Olay brand or buying in (at great expense) a credible skincare brand.

The next stage is to then flesh out these simple choices by looking at the possible options that deliver against the choice.

In the research, Lafley et al talked about options of expanding Oil of Olay in its current niche or moving it into a higher price point.

P&G did not ignore other creative options, however. The company also considered moving the Cover Girl brand into skincare as an alternative to the initial choices.

For each choice, P&G would define the possibility that the option might succeed and explain the nuances of each possibility. That would mean describing each possibility in a realistic but optimistic way as if it had already succeeded – painting the picture of that success in terms of the competitive advantage, scope where the advantage is real and finally the activities needed throughout the company to deliver the possibility. Lafley refers to these possibilities as 'happy stories'.

I'll admit that sounds a bit, erm... Well it doesn't sound great. But the underlying theory is important. You're looking at a definition of a reasonable, optimistic outcome for the business (based on a particular premise) that they fleshed out before settling on their final choice. One benefit is that the expansion of the original premise also gives you a plan of what you need to change, gaps you need to fill, things to do, etc. That's what you will then be testing.

P&G came up with five of these 'strategic possibilities' in the end.

CREATING STRATEGIC POSSIBILITIES

You want to have the right team working on this approach. That means getting people from across the business to ensure that you have a broad perspective on potential choices. If not, you risk having too narrow a focus.

An important part of the process follows the rules of brainstorming. Generating ideas needs to be separated from the evaluation and selection process. Otherwise you risk killing good ideas before you've even started.

If this becomes impossible, for example if someone just keeps going on about some potential hurdle, the constraint needs to be rephrased as a condition that must be met. So if someone in the team keeps saying that a customer segment won't go for a lower quality product, this can become a condition such as, "The strategic possibility requires customers in the segment to be willing to purchase a lower quality variant."

However, the similarity to brainstorming rules described above doesn't mean that all the relevant ideas can or should be found in one focused session. The strategy team should be open to these possibilities evolving over a period and not artificially limit the scope of options considered by rushing the process.

You can apply this structured approach as follows.

1. Frame two or more mutually exclusive choices for the organization going forward

2. Recognizing a choice needs to be made, you now flesh out the choices with further relevant choices
3. Define the conditions. Answer the question: 'What has to be true for this possibility to make logical sense?' You're creating a logic tree by answering that question. There will probably be multiple factors and for each one that would need to be true, a line is drawn fanning out from a point (the root if you like) to the right of the page.

   Each assumption is written at the right hand end of its own line.

   Then you repeat the process but asking that same question: 'what has to be true for this to make logical sense?' for every assumption you've just written.

   Each time you drill down into an assumption, it adds more detail.
4. Identify barriers. Define which conditions are least likely to be true.
5. Design tests. For each of the barrier conditions, figure out the way in which you will test it in a sufficiently robust manner so that people will agree on the findings.
6. Carry out the tests
7. Use the test results to initially reduce down the number of choices and ultimately select the most appropriate choice based on the results of the tests.

One key option to consider is the 'do nothing' strategy or 'steady as she goes'. This means carrying on with the current strategy (or absence of strategy). To be clear, this doesn't mean nothing will change for the company. You have to do the work to understand what will happen to markets, revenues, margins, etc. if you stay on your current course. This provides a vital baseline against which you can then compare the other options.

The evaluation and selection process is worth looking at in slightly more detail. Essentially, you are looking to work to reverse-engineer the conditions that will need to be true for the strategic possibility to be successful.

A more specific set of conditions can be developed by using a framework that considers different parts of the organization's ecosystem. This is not necessarily exhaustive but you can add to this list as you see fit or as you think better suits your own organization.

For this strategic option to be true...

Business area	Detailed area	What must be true
Competition	Competitors	How must competitors react?
Business model	Capabilities	What must be true about our capabilities and how should these capabilities compare to our competitors?
	Costs	What must be true about our costs and how should these compare to our competitors?
Customers	Channel	What must the channel value?
	Customers	What must the customers value?
Industry	Segmentation	How must the market be segmented?
	Structure	How attractive must the segments be?

So what are the big takeaways here?

- **In Good to Great terms, get the 'right people on the bus' with you for this exercise.** Assemble the right people in a team with you and then concentrate on defining realistic but relevant strategic possibilities.
- **'What must be true for this strategic possibility to be true?'.** If you find the right possibilities and frame the questions well, it will carefully help direct the work you need to do (and what you don't).
- **This is a creative process.** In part that requires management of disbelief and criticism. Strategy should be looking beyond the mundane and simple because even if something looks hard it should not be dismissed. Remember, if you can define the conditions that need to be satisfied for a potential

strategy to be valid, you focus on what needs to be true, not what is difficult. This gets you thinking about the 'how' of the situation. This has to be true so 'how' can we make it true? What do we need to do so that it is true?

Source

Lafley, A. G. & Martin, Roger L., *Playing to Win: How Strategy Really Works* (Harvard Business Review Press, Boston, 2013)

See also

Read Chapter 24 if you haven't already. It provides an alternative view on creating a new business model.

Further reading

Kim, W. Chan & Mauborgne, Renée, *Blue Ocean Strategy: How to Create Uncontested Market Space and Make the Competition Irrelevant* (Harvard Business Review Press, Boston, 2005)

30 HOW STRATEGY SHAPES STRUCTURE

Drive your situation rather than the situation driving you

Kim and Mauborgne talk about what they call the 'structuralist' approach to strategy that has been in place for several decades.

This means, look at the external environment, consider your competitors, buyers, suppliers, etc., think about the strengths and weaknesses of the organization and seek to find competitive advantages that you can exploit in the market. The strategy is a product of the environment or, put another way, 'structure shapes strategy'.

The researchers' view is that some companies follow the reverse process, and they call this Blue Ocean Strategy. The metaphor of blue ocean means finding the water not churned up by others. It's your own piece of territory to exploit. That's at the heart of the Blue Ocean Strategy. It's about setting a strategy that will define or redefine the environment. Instead of a structuralist, 'outside-in' approach, this is a reconstructionist approach.

Modern examples of this might be Airbnb or Uber, who have completely overturned the traditional models for delivery of accommodation and taxis respectively. There's probably not a better pair of examples, since these two have changed their markets forever in spite of their singular lack of either hotel rooms or taxis respectively.

Kim and Mauborgne suggest that structuralist approaches still have a place, which is a relief given how much this book discusses them, but they believe the reconstructionist approach will be a better alternative under some circumstances.

In order to decide which of the two alternatives will be more appropriate, you need to look at three things.

The first are the conditions the organization is working within. The second relates to the capabilities and skills available in the organization and the final aspect is the strategic mindset.

Conditions

This is about whether the conditions driven by the business environment for the organization are favourable or not.

Capabilities and resources

You need to consider the strengths and/or weaknesses of the capabilities and resources in relation to the external conditions.

Strategic mindset

This is perhaps simplistic but is about whether your organization is biased towards innovation and exploiting new opportunities or is more defensively minded around current markets/products.

In addition to the interaction between these three attributes, Kim and Mauborgne discussed the need to have three parts of the overall strategic propositions for the organization as follows:

- A value proposition that attracts buyers
- A profit proposition that means the company makes money from the value proposition
- A people proposition that encourages the right behaviour from those within the company to deliver the strategy. This will impact on how well the company executes.

They therefore define strategy as the creation and alignment of these three propositions to exploit or reconstruct the industry and economic environment in which the organization functions.

As a simple example of bad alignment in the three propositions mentioned above, you could raise revenues dramatically by slashing prices below cost. This would probably drive a big jump in terms of market share, which you might enjoy only briefly since you're likely to go out of business quite rapidly. The value proposition looks great for buyers but the profit proposition has evaporated in this case.

Kim and Mauborgne believe that if you don't get a good and consistent set of propositions, you are doomed to do badly in terms of financial performance and/or execution.

So let's consider how the structuralist and reconstructionist approaches differ in terms of these propositions.

In a **structuralist approach,** you are likely to be defining the propositions to be consistent around either a low-cost or differentiation-based approach (as defined in Chapter 12 on building competitive advantage). That means all three of the different propositions aiming for low cost or differentiation – not any kind of mix. A low-cost value proposition may not be achievable if the people proposition is all about differentiation. The latter means you may have more expensive people who are more attuned to customer intimacy and service than being profitable in a low-cost situation.

In a **reconstructionist strategic approach,** you are looking to define the three propositions to pursue both low cost and differentiation. This should enable it to create that 'clear blue water' for itself to exploit in a market. The belief is that it's harder to imitate all three of the propositions to catch up. Strategy is now shaping structure.

Kim and Mauborgne's work shows how a misalignment across the three propositions can lead to failure. Twitter has a huge valuation but has it figured out its value proposition yet? Having lots of members/users is seen as very valuable as you should be able to use them for something (e.g. sell them something, gather data from them, advertise to them) but I'd suggest Twitter hasn't nailed down the value aspect of the propositions yet.

Dyson produced a brilliant contra-rotating washing machine as a result of smart people, well-motivated, etc. (meaning good people and resources/capabilities propositions), allied to a shaky value proposition. The washing machine was very good but not good enough (in the minds of potential customers, which is where it counts) to justify a very high price. Luckily, Dyson wasn't affected too badly by this relative failure.

WHICH APPROACH TO USE?

In the face of the potential variations in these three attributes, Kim and Mauborgne have defined a simple set of rules for choosing the right approach to developing strategy in an organization.

Structuralist approaches work well when...	Reconstructionist approaches work well when...
Structural conditions are favourable for the organization and it has the resources and capabilities to create a strongly competitive position	Structural conditions are favourable but the competition is strongly entrenched and the organization does not have the resources and capabilities to de-position or outperform the competitors
Structural conditions are less than favourable for the organization but it has the resources and capabilities to do better than the competition	Structural conditions are poor for the organization and regardless of the resources and capabilities in the organization
Structural conditions and the match to resources and capabilities are not particularly in favour for either approach. The choice will then be based on the mindset of the organization.	
The organization is more defensively minded and is reluctant to go into new market/ product areas	The organization is biased towards innovation and finding new sources of revenue

So the first stage for a strategic review is to assess which approach you are going to take to strategy. This is not something that should be taken lightly and for larger organizations it may be that different business units will make different choices about which approach is right for them.

Once this choice has been made, the next part is to start to develop the three strategic propositions (value, profit and people). The challenge for senior management is to ensure that whichever approach is taken, the distinction between low cost or differentiation (structuralist) or low cost and differentiation (reconstructionist) is followed through.

As outline propositions are considered, they should be reviewed and refined in terms of:

- their fit to the situation (environment, resources, capabilities)
- consistency with the other strategic propositions
- delivery against one or both of low cost and differentiation positions depending on the choice of strategic approach.

So what are the big takeaways here?

- **Confront the truth of your situation.** Be clear and honest about where you sit in relation to the environment, your skills and level of ambition in the business. Any error here will mean you get the right result but based on an incorrect set of assumptions.
- **Choose and improve the best propositions.** In particular for the blue ocean, reconstructionist approach you need to keep asking if the set of three propositions is going to deliver both low cost and differentiation. If not, you may be deluding yourself about how unique the position will be and how long it will take to imitate.
- **Relaxing is unlikely to ever be an option.** You may have to become more innovative and future market focused if your current market is going away. It may not be the 'nature' of the organization now but if the environment demands innovation from you, there is no point sticking to a relentlessly defensive mindset. If that's the case, you may find yourself defending nothing at all in the end.

Source

Kim, W. Chan & Mauborgne, Renée, *Blue Ocean Strategy: How to Create Uncontested Market Space and Make the Competition Irrelevant* (Harvard Business Review Press, Boston, 2005)

See also

The strategy and business model are inextricably linked. To fully understand the context here, read the next chapter that is going to expand on business model thinking.

Further reading

Lafley, A. G. & Martin, Roger L., *Playing to Win: How Strategy Really Works* (Harvard Business Review Press, Boston, 2013)

31 GETTING THE BUSINESS MODEL RIGHT

Getting to the right level of business model innovation

The research starts with feedback from IBM's Institute for Business Value's Global CEO Study. Reassuringly, it suggested in 2009 that 7 out of 10 companies were looking to create innovative business models with 98 per cent of them modifying their underlying business model as a result. It doesn't talk about the success or otherwise of these changes or how committed the businesses really are to the changes. You can imagine some of them are saying the right things and not really following through. However, it's encouraging to see this kind of response as businesses face tougher competition and increasing difficulties in creating and maintaining competitive advantages.

So let's start by coming up with a definition of a business model. But there are lots of definitions around and a lack of agreement on one definition. Here's mine for what it's worth:

'An integrated plan for the successful delivery of the different objectives of the business – defining the situation, challenges, markets, revenues, customers, products/services and the budget that underpins it all.'

The business model should answer a number of questions such as providing an integrated approach to the delivery of the value, profit and people propositions (see Chapter 30 for more on this).

It might sound like a business plan but a business model encompasses all the processes and operational aspects that aren't captured in an Excel spreadsheet or Word document.

The IBM research identifies a couple of serious weaknesses in the way that companies create their own business models. For example, one issue is that many business models are created in isolation – failing to consider competitors' own business models and how these will interact with one another. In addition, what are the likely competitive responses to any change in business model? Assuming you can have it all your own way is short-sighted and likely to lead to painful mistakes.

The second shortfall of most business models is that they do not act to gain competitive advantage for the organization. This is a much more subtle point so let's look at this in more detail.

Casadesus-Masanell and Ricart suggest that a business model at its simplest will effectively pair choices with consequences. It's classic cause and effect.

The choices have three dimensions:

- **Policies** (e.g. manufacture locally or in low-cost countries)
- **Assets** (how the company chooses to use the assets at its disposal)
- **Governance** (how the decision-making works across the first two).

The choices made across the three areas will give rise to either flexible or rigid consequences.

The authors use low-cost airline Ryanair's generic approach to business as an example but perhaps a more up to date and relevant aspect of the company's business model is the effort to seduce business travellers. It is advertising about the punctuality of its services, etc. and hoping this sways business travellers away from more traditional airlines. Think about that for a second. Ryanair's business model has been built on being low cost and it has almost wilfully seemed to avoid being seen as customer friendly at every turn. It's timekeeping claims about 'on time arrivals' are not measured by monitoring organization IATA (like other airlines) and so perhaps carry less weight. Finally, and perhaps most damaging to its ambitions in driving to be low cost, it has set up in airports some distance away from city centres. Business people presumably will be less happy to have to take a longer journey in to their destination. There's plainly a mismatch.

So you could argue that the choices Ryanair has made are now acting directly against its ability to attract significant numbers of business passengers.

However, its traditional business model has served it well.

The diagram below shows a 'strategy map' that outlines some aspects of the low-cost airline business model and the interactions across different parts of the business – in Balanced Scorecard style (see Chapter 39 for more on this).

Airlines put in policies to have non-unionized workers and so have more flexibility about what they can be asked to do. You can see how that flexibility can lead to increased usage of their main asset (the planes) leading to lower costs, more passengers and more profit (if done correctly).

The researchers talk about such interactions and the creation of virtuous cycles. The ability to be low cost creates attractive prices that bring in more customers who increase the load factor (percentage of seats filled) per plane, increasing revenue per flight, allowing costs to be further reduced, attracting more customers, etc. That's a virtuous cycle right there!

If a low-cost airline tries to become a premium carrier, some of the policy choices that helped make it effective as a low-cost player are likely to now act against it. We can see this from Ryanair, where the choice of lower-cost locations means the airports are more distant from city centres.

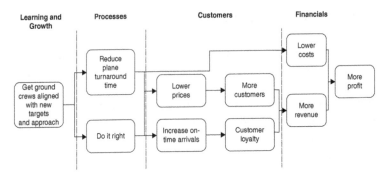

Figure 31.1 An example of a strategy map for a low-cost airline

DO POTENTIAL BUSINESS MODELS FIT?

To check if the business model is appropriate, you can look at three dimensions.

Does the business model align with the company's goals?

This is another way of repeating one of the themes of this book – consistency and alignment with what you want to achieve and how you plan to get there.

Is the model self-reinforcing?

This is another way of considering the fit between the value proposition, profit proposition and people proposition (as described in Chapter 30). If you're trying to charge a premium but are set up for low-cost labour in customer-facing positions, you're likely to suffer because of this mismatch.

Is it resilient and robust?

There are four threats, defined by strategist Pankaj Ghemawat, that the model should be able to withstand.

- **Imitation** – how easily and quickly can your business model be copied?
- **Holdup** – can suppliers hijack your profit proposition by holding you to ransom (e.g. if they are a sole supplier of a vital component)?

- **Slack** – does the organization care enough or work hard enough?
- **Substitution** – do other products/services exist that could erode/destroy customers' view of the value of your products?

If you understand the answers to these points, a company can use the business model to compete aggressively through three components.

Strengthen the virtuous cycle

Investment in flexible manufacturing allows carmakers to base multiple models on a single platform. VW has been able to use one car platform (MQB) to deliver 43 different car variants across VW, SEAT, Audi and Skoda brands. Each additional car that is based on the platform helps spread the development cost across more models and hence reduces the cost to produce an individual model. This leads to sales success and/or improved margins but the increased volumes also should deliver economies of scale that further enhance costs/margins. VW's virtuous cycle in this area has enabled it to out-compete some competitors. Ulrich Hackenberg, Head of VW's R&D department, called the platform 'a strategic weapon'.

Weaken competitors' cycles

As an example of this, Intel has the potential to fight very hard against rival ARM by leveraging the breadth of offerings it has for OEM manufacturers of electronics. It could do a bundle deal with mobile processors (where ARM is very strong) priced aggressively low while making better margins on processors for laptops (where ARM is weaker).

Turn competitors into complements

This is a harder one to get right as essentially you're looking for someone else to grow the market on your behalf. The premium headphone market has probably benefited disproportionately from the growth in smartphones and tablets, even though the device manufacturers often bundle headphones with the device and may even have their own line of headphones. As to whether that's a happy accident or by design is perhaps open to question.

A different example would be something I worked on, looking at two small operators entering the mobile market. They had to build their own networks but would do better financially if they shared the network capital expenses. Although in theory they are rivals, they would actually do better by cooperating on the infrastructure at the start. Neither has any subscribers to start with so they can't take customers from each other. Even if they achieved 5 per cent market share each (a realistic target), the vast majority of customers they could win would be from other companies – not each other. So, they can consider cooperation as a valid option.

So what are the big takeaways here?

- **Business is like a boxing match.** No opponent stands still and lets you hit them. They react, counter-punch, surprise you, launch counter-attacks, move, bob, weave, etc. Your business model needs to consider the reaction of your competitors.
- **Does it fit you like a glove?** Now you may need to change resources, balance of personnel, skills, etc. over time, but as you consider the organization, the business model should fit you really well (and leverage unique aspects of your business).
- **Attack and attack.** Improve your own model to lock people in, give them more behefits, lower their costs to deal with you, respond faster or whatever will keep them working with you, buying from you, supplying to you, etc. In parallel, look to weaken the way your competition operates by using bespoke systems, sharing your facilities or any other approach that makes it less attractive for people to work with, or buy from your competitors.

Sources

Casadesus-Masanell, R. & Ricart, J. E., 'Competing Through Business Models', IESE Business School, November 2007
http://www.iese.edu/research/pdfs/DI-0713-E.pdf

Casadesus-Masanell, R. & Ricart, J. E., 'How to Design a Winning Business Model', *Harvard Business Review*, January 2011

See also

Chapter 30 – Fleshes out the thinking about the different propositions that need to be created and harmonized.

Chapter 39 – Describes the balanced scorecard methodology that links strategy to consistent metrics.

Further reading

Kaplan, Robert S. & Norton, David P., *The Balanced Scorecard* (Harvard Business Review Press, Boston, 1996)

Pride comes before a fall – and so can over-ambition!

Jim Collins wrote *Good to Great*. If you ever want to read a good book on business... start there. And I mean that. The very first book on the list.

In *Great by Choice*, written with Morten Hansen, he has carried on from *Good to Great* and studied what they called '10X' companies. These are ones that have outperformed their market or competition by a factor of ten. One good thing about this work is that hindsight often helps strategic thinkers refine their thinking (as in this case) or occasionally be discredited by time and the failure of the heroes of their thinking (not the case with Jim Collins). However Collins and Hansen also took on an extra dimension with this book by targeting high-performing businesses in extreme environments. This reflected the increasingly turbulent era in which businesses are struggling to thrive. The successful cases all began as immature companies or from a relatively weak market position and had to become great over at least 15 years to be studied.

So, importantly, Collins and Hansen did not select firms that might appear in a 'flavour of the month' management book.

The relatively few companies that met their challenging criteria included perennial management book favourite, Southwest Airlines, as well as Microsoft and Intel alongside other less well-known companies. It should be noted the lessons learned were up to 2002 but because the markets were highly turbulent (apologies for that given we're talking about an airline), they remain valid examples of the difficulties and choices faced today.

For each 10X company, they then studied the approach and performance of a shadow company in the same sector that had not done as well. I won't mention that Microsoft has Apple as its 'poor relation' or you might spit coffee over the pages. Just bear with me. This is useful thinking.

Collins and Hansen used 7,000 pieces of company information in their study and came up with some interesting conclusions.

Conventional wisdom	Findings
Successful leadership in super-dynamic markets requires boldness and a willingness to take risks allied to the skill to see into the future	The best leaders were not visionaries as such but instead identified what works, why it works and then how to do it more
The 10X companies would be innovation led and set apart by the quality of this innovation	Although the 10X companies did innovate, the distinguishing feature was more their ability to combine that innovation with the capacity to scale up around it. They tied together innovation and business discipline There is a threshold level of innovation needed to participate in a market (like the idea of meeting qualifying criteria in a sales process), but above this level, additional innovation did not seem to produce incremental benefits
Move fast or die	Choose when to go fast wisely. Blind pursuit of fast everything is not the way
You need to be lucky	The 10X companies were not intrinsically luckier than the lesser ones. It's not about good luck or bad luck – it's what you do with both

On that last point, the authors were very clear indeed in their derision of relying on luck. This is similar to Richard Rumelt's scorn for New Age thinking where your will can help manifest results. These researchers are all more grounded in Gary Player's 'the more I practice, the luckier I get' school of thinking (and the more practical and pragmatic for it).

One aspect of the successful companies revolved around the concept of what the authors call 'The 20-Mile [http://www.jimcollins.com/article_topics/articles/how-to-manage-through-chaos.html] March'. This metaphor reflects a view of slower but steady, almost metronomic progress towards objectives. The time taken for each '20 miles' should be planned carefully but the key principle is that you are trying to find ways to grow but without failing by overstretching. That failure may occur in terms of the finance available to support the business (over-trading) or delivery (shortages, quality problems), etc. Either way, you're searching for growth within your organization's capabilities.

Now this might seem counterintuitive or at least a bit underwhelming in the turbulent environments they are addressing and that you and I see around us. However, this approach creates a baseline of expectation of success, reduces the chance of catastrophic cock-up and helps build confidence in the organization.

Interestingly, this metaphor from one person's trans-American walk (20 miles per day) was later identified as underpinning Amundsen's successful approach to getting to the South Pole. In contrast, the intrepid Scott's less constrained approach had variable distance targets each day and sometimes ended days with his team exhausted. Of course there's more ins and outs to that story but you get the point.

BALANCING YOUR AMBITION

The 20-Mile March thoughts get you thinking around a few concepts.

First, you have to work hard in tough times to hit these targets. However, perhaps more difficult is some measure of restraint when things are good. Serious cyclists reading this know the uphill bit is where you can lose your competition but you also have to survive the downhill sections without crashing in order to win the race.

In setting this type of control, you should look for seven things:

1. Clear indicators – so you know how you're doing against some minimum standards of performance
2. Constraints set by you – to limit your ambition
3. Customization to the organization and the environment it's operating within
4. The ambitions should be within your control – no luck required, no Big Hairy Audacious Goals present
5. The right time frame for the march – too short and it becomes meaningless, too long and it doesn't motivate or drive the organization
6. Designed and enforced by the organization itself. You have to own it!
7. Consistency, consistency, consistency. Results matter, intentions don't.

The authors come up with a lovely phrase to describe the way that the 10X companies did some of their innovation. Bullets then cannonballs… This means not throwing the kitchen sink at every situation. Instead, they looked to make a proportionate initial investment that combined low cost (for the company's size), low risk (limiting the company's exposure if it all goes horribly wrong) and low distraction. That last one is interesting since the approach to disruptive technologies and business models suggests a separate organization for a number of reasons and this separation can also limit any unnecessary distraction for the main company.

As a final thought, the authors also discuss some helpfully paranoid viewpoints that may help an organization. I like paranoid thinking at times as a smack on the side of the head to force you to aggressively think about how things might go wrong, rather than assuming they'll go right. The suggestions (and I've seen businesses die simply for ignoring the first and focusing too hard on revenue growth) are:

- Build cash reserves (or save for a rainy day as an elderly relative might have told you once)
- Limit your exposure to risk with specific limits including time

frames for decision making. Treat these as hard limits and respect them.

- Zoom in and zoom out – or chunk up and down as a cognitive psychologist might say. Manage the detail obsessively but be able to get a helicopter view to keep on top of whether your situation and approach are still relevant.

So what are the big takeaways here?

- **Slow and steady wins the race.** Okay we're not talking about going too slowly but the steady part is key. Constraining your ambition when times are good, and going hard when times are tougher can keep momentum in the business without too much risk.
- **Bullets then cannonballs.** That's a great phrase that mimics thoughts in a number of chapters in the book. Failure is not something to avoid at all costs. You're trying to take enough risk but do so in a smart way. Using bullets (smaller initial investments of time and resources) to check you're on target makes sense. When you have more information and certainty, you start with the cannonballs.
- **Scaling smart ideas wins.** It's the ability to scale up innovations that will make the important difference here. Bright ideas alone are not enough.

Sources

Collins, Jim & Hansen, Morten T., *Great by Choice: Uncertainty, Chaos and Luck - Why Some Thrive Despite Them All* (Harper Business, New York, 2011)

See also

In a similar vein, have a read of Chapter 36 if you want some clear and pithy views on what is important in developing strategy.

Further reading

Rumelt, Richard, *Good Strategy/Bad Strategy* (Profile Books, London, 2012)

33 BEYOND A SIMPLE BUSINESS MODEL – REAL OPTION PRICING

Intelligent management of upside opportunities and downside risks

The problem with business models created in Excel can be their apparent air of precision. You can have incredibly clever formulae and hundreds of assumptions all combining to produce numbers to a high number of decimal places. This doesn't make them right. This just makes them look convincing.

Mikael Collan, Professor of Strategic Finance at Lappeenranta University of Technology in Finland, proposed an approach beyond the limitations of single scenario, discounted cash flow based models (and the myriad sensitivity cases that are then developed around them).

Before going on to discuss his approach, let's pause to understand the problem.

What I'll call static business modelling generates a specific financial result for a given set of assumptions. That might be an Internal Rate of Return (IRR) or a Net Present Value (NPV) that should, if done correctly, reflect the expected situation. Now these models are the result of a set of variables where one 'expected' value is chosen for each assumption and you consider the flow of cash in and out, year by year before coming up with some answers as to whether this is a good potential investment or not.

In simple terms, think about modelling your journey somewhere. You might have experience of the range of times certain parts of it have taken in the past. However, in the end you take a guess at the overall duration based on assumptions for each leg of the journey.

We do the same with business models. Estimate the overall market size, think about a company's share and revenues and define how these may change over time. This and a hundred other things may easily impact the revenue estimates. To balance this out, you then estimate the cost side for capital and operating expenditures, finance costs, tax, cash flow, etc. It all seems very reassuring in the detail it provides.

However, go back to that journey you planned again. You have made an estimate that ignores the full amount of information you had. Your expected journey time may well represent the most likely outcome, but there will be other possible outcomes.

For example, if it was definitely your day, you might find every leg of the journey was the shortest you had ever experienced. You know, every light is green all the way. You step onto the platform and board the train just as it departs. However, that's fairly unlikely. Chances are at least one leg will be screwed up on the way.

Then there is the opposite extreme. You probably wouldn't expect every part of the journey to be the worst it's ever been. But it might be.

In between these two extremes, you'll find a range of journey times that essentially you have ignored.

The same thing happens with business models. So think about what they then do to try to get some comfort that the model and numbers are robust. Teams pore over the numbers and use sensitivity analyses to try to consider what might go wrong.

You'll frequently see people taking sales figures down 10 per cent or costs up 10 per cent and seeing what the impact is on the numbers. What's so great about 10 per cent? For some business models that will be far too high, and for others will fail to match the potential variation in results that may occur.

It doesn't consider the inherent risk in the model and so is unlikely to give results that accurately reflect the range of possible outcomes.

A SMARTER WAY TO ASSESSING OPPORTUNITIES

So what's the answer?

The concept of real option pricing is simple at heart – then the maths gets a bit more intimidating so let's keep it simple for now. As discussed above, there is a range of potential outcomes for a business strategy that could, for example, be characterized as different combinations of price vs volume.

The next diagram is pretty complicated at first glance but I'll explain and I think you'll find it is actually quite straightforward.

First look at the curve. If you reduce the price for something, you can imagine the volume of it will rise. If you increase the price, the volume is likely to reduce.

The curve shows that effect in action with the vertical axis showing price and the horizontal axis showing volume. The sensitivity to price in a market (the 'price elasticity') will change the shape of this curve but that's not important here. Just assume the curve above is an accurate representation for a given market.

Now there are two extreme positions on the curve. You'll see that positions beyond each point are shown, but the extreme points have been chosen for a reason. They represent the best possible and worst possible cases. However, in both instances, these cases should be reasonable. Though they show optimistic and pessimistic cases, these must be ones that could happen. If not, results of the modelling will be skewed or even completely erroneous.

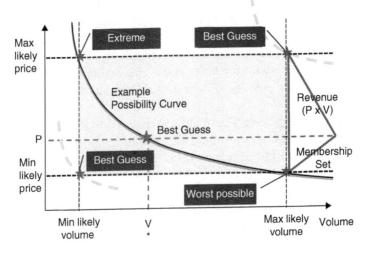

Figure 33.1 The Real Option Model approach

Note the combination of results that provide these two cases. The best case is the highest price and lowest volume case. Volume will relate to costs so the best case is one where you achieve the high income with only low output needed to produce it. The worst case is the reverse. In that instance, the case reflects the lowest income requiring the highest volume to deliver it (and hence costs).

So there is a potential range of results between the extremes of the best and worst case.

The position of the expected result (the Best Guess) adds information about the distribution of these. For example, in the picture there is more upside on price than downside and vice versa for volume.

In the metaphor of a journey, your expected time might be only ten minutes below the minimum journey time but hours less than the maximum possible time. In that case, you'd have to be concerned that many more of the different journey times possible are above your expected time.

The possibility set (shown as a simple triangle to the right of the curve in the diagram) maps the full range of possible solutions and is used to drive the calculation of fuzzy logic based calculations. It should reflect the full business context and the extreme positions for other underlying assumptions in the model to create possible and reasonable best and worst cases.

From this point, I'm going to gloss over the mathematics. It's like time travel in a film, sometimes it's best just to go with the flow so take my word for it that maths is then applied to convert the overall probability set into a set of results.

The first is the Base Case result that reflects the Net Present Value that you would achieve if you modelled the Best Guess set of assumptions in the traditional way.

The next important value is the Real Option Value. This reflects not just the point result for the Best Guess but combines it with analysis of the full probability set. Look at the diagram that follows. It shows a probability set that is mainly above the Base Case or Best Guess result that is shown as the zero point on here. The Real Option Value is therefore above the Base Case NPV.

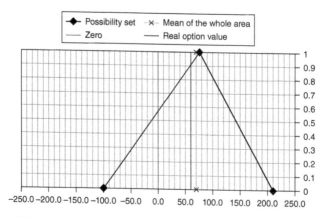

Figure 33.2 An example of the output from a real option exercise

So what are the big takeaways here?

- **Standard business cases can be over-reliant on the assumptions.** As a minimum case, you need to ensure that those assumptions are as accurate as they can be. Doing sensitivity analysis can provide comfort that you understand what will happen if things go well or badly but they tend to consist of changing just one variable and so do not sufficiently portray what may happen.
- **A real option approach is more complex but is better.** Real options take account of the spread of potential outcomes and can provide greater information about the outcomes.

Source

Collan, Mikael, *The Pay-off Method* – Re-Inventing [https://www.createspace.com/3936428] *Investment Analysis* (CreateSpace, 2012)

See also

The business cases in your own company and the sensitivity analyses done around them. Once you've read this chapter you'll perhaps recognize some of the limitations in those cases.

Further reading

You can read more about investment appraisal approaches (and limitations) in:

Jones, Richard A. D., *One Day MBA: Skills For Succeeding in Business Today* (Winmark/ICSA, London, 2012)

34 FINDING THE RIGHT BALANCE FOR INNOVATION

How much innovation is enough and in which areas?

As we watch the rate of change increasing in different industries and business models changing out of all recognition in only a few years, it is important to understand that innovation has a place at the heart of every business. Without innovation, evolving customer demands and competing offers will weaken any advantages a company may have until those advantages, and maybe the company itself, no longer exist.

Bansi Nagji and Geoff Tuff looked at the way companies operate in terms of innovation. They assessed the balance between different types of innovation in a search for the magic ratio. They think they found it! More of that in a while but let's look at some of the other findings first before explaining their definitions and findings.

Their first simple finding resonates throughout this book.

Disconnected pockets of innovation do not constitute a strategy.

Stop and think for a moment. Apple is spending around US$6 billion a year on R&D. Is that enough or is it too much? What will be more important is where that is being spent. What does Apple need? Lots of incremental development of existing products or creation of new ones? How about brand new technologies or approaches to underpin new products? What's the balance between software and hardware? What should they do themselves and what should they outsource? What do they need to invest for the near term and what needs to be done for longer-term success?

Every company has to think about the same problem – the search for the best use of their finite resources.

There are a few different descriptions of the types of innovation that a company can pursue. For example, Jean-Philippe Deschamps talks about core, differentiating, pacing and emerging as follows:

- **Core** – fundamental aspect of how a product or service operates today (and assumed to be shared by everyone)
- **Differentiating** – how a product or service is differentiated in the mind of the customer
- **Pacing** – a technology/approach that looks likely to become a differentiating factor in the future
- **Emerging** – similar to pacing but things in this category may become differentiating in the future – or may equally disappear.

Nagji and Tuff's categorization is similar. They talk about core, adjacent and transformational initiatives within a company as a means to deliver against a clear innovation strategy.

Their Innovation Ambition Matrix is a clever variation of the Ansoff Matrix, below.

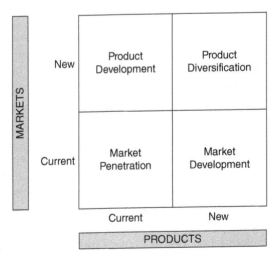

Figure 34.1 The Ansoff Matrix

Ansoff defined the four areas that you could exploit to generate new revenues. The words in the box are the generic actions you need to undertake for each area. The choice about which areas you move to (from your current market and product/service) is an important one.

The authors in this case see **Core Innovations** as the improvement of existing products for existing customers. In Ansoff terms, that is the market penetration area where you're trying to increase revenues by selling to more customers in your core markets.

Adjacent Innovation aims to move the business into 'new to the company' areas. To be clear, that means that although the new revenues are coming from areas that are new to the company, there are other companies that are already exploiting these areas. This means practically that the risk is not too great as there is revenue potential there.

Transformational Innovation means working to deliver to markets that don't currently exist.

An overall strategy needs to cascade down into consistent strategies within the business that will deliver in their particular area.

The results suggested that, on average, companies outperforming their peers were investing in the three areas **with 70 per cent in Core, 20 per cent in Adjacent and 10 per cent in Transformational.** However those figures are the average and will vary by sector.

Although those figures may be correct for a diversified industrials company, **a leading FMCG company was closer to 80 per cent Core, 18 per cent Adjacent and 2 per cent Transformational.** The reasoning for this latter breakdown could be that the potential for real, groundbreaking innovation is far less in this sector.

A mid-stage technology firm was closer to **45 per cent Core, 40 per cent Adjacent and 15 per cent Transformational.** This can be seen as reflecting the need to come up with the next 'big thing' for the sector.

A second dimension that would affect the 'correct' balance was the competitive positioning of the company. A laggard might want to bet big on transformational innovation to try to leapfrog the leader.

A final dimension that will affect the mix of innovation efforts is the maturity of the company. The more mature, the lower the tendency might be to go for the big gamble on transformation.

The bottom line is that the management of the company needs to get the ratio right and recognize the optimum blend will change over time.

SO HOW DO YOU RESPOND?

The first step should be to understand the current situation in terms of investment into the different innovation categories. This should combine both the financial investment (by year) and also the likely duration of the project. In this, assess the balance of the current portfolio.

In their book *Product Juggernauts*, Deschamps and Nayak proposed options for companies to consider in terms of their response to competition as follows:

- Target and Beat
- Target and Emulate
- Monitor Carefully
- Cooperate.

If you've decided on responses based on these categories, you can start to understand what you should be doing in terms of innovation. That will provide you with a target balance in the innovation portfolio between the different types.

However, in the real world you will need to have a form of Stage-Gate® process (see Chapter 23) to ensure that, month by month, you are adding new projects to the portfolio of innovation projects that are consistent with your target mix. You can't just mindlessly add projects as you'll end up with a balance of investment a long way from what you're looking for.

A serious challenge can be that the skills required for the different types of innovation are not the same.

For Core and Adjacent innovation, the team suggests that a high degree of analysis is required to interpret customer and market information.

Transformational innovation is about areas that do not exist at this point and so deep analysis is impossible. For these innovations, the skills required are more about creation of new ideas as well as tracking technologies to formulate and evaluate new product/service configurations.

So your organization also needs to be configured to provide the resources needed for each of these different innovation types. That will impact structure, training and recruitment over time.

So what is the big takeaway here?

One size does not fit all. You need to understand the current mix of innovation investments. Then ensure that you move to the right mix for the future. That means understanding the current portfolio and how each potential new project will impact that.

Sources

Deschamps, Jean-Philippe, Nayak, P. Ranganath, *Product Juggernauts: How Companies Mobilize to Generate a Stream of Market Winners* (Harvard Business School Press and Arthur D. Little Inc., 1995)

Nagji, B. & Tuff, G., 'Managing Your Innovation Portfolio', *Harvard Business Review*, May 2012

See also

Chapter 35 – Provides a different view of innovation from the perspective of someone with an idea. It develops some approaches on how to get backing for a good idea.

Further reading

The Ansoff Matrix and details of portfolio management are outlined in the following book:

Jones, Richard A. D., *One Day MBA: Skills For Succeeding in Business Today* (Winmark/ICSA, London, 2012)

THE CASE FOR STEALTH INNOVATION

Why getting early backing from the top might be the wrong approach for innovative ideas

Paddy Miller and Thomas Wedell-Wedellsborg put forward a viewpoint that innovators traditionally are counselled to go the top of the organization to gain support. After all, if the CEO loves an idea, who of all the naysayers and 'not invented here' merchants will be able to oppose it?

There are two potential pitfalls of this approach.

The first is that a time-poor CEO gives a great idea the full two minutes consideration (if that) and then dismisses it – never realizing the lost opportunity that has passed.

The second problem is that an idea may get too much attention early on. If you've ever explained a complex concept to someone, you'll be familiar with the frustration that sometimes they forget all the nuances, caveats and downsides you set out. People may remember just the upside and good news about an idea while forgetting the rest. Expectations may be too high and when a small but natural setback occurs, confidence in the idea may be undermined completely.

They talk about learning from working with innovative managers who have developed alternative approaches to progressing ideas.

As one example, they discuss pfizerWorks. In a step somewhat related to Jack Welch's 'Work-Out' process changes at General Electric, the pfizerWorks concept was that 'grunt work' would be outsourced to stop it eating into the valuable time of the Pfizer employees. Even though groups in the company had to pay for this service out of their own budgets, it became the most popular service offering according to an internal survey in 2011.

Jordan Cohen had the idea but didn't rush to senior management. Instead, he went into stealth mode for a year while the service concept was developed, supporters were found and evidence gathered. When he finally put his head above the parapet with the idea, it was supported by ambassadors within the management team. Support for the idea from the top then appeared quickly.

OUT IN THE OPEN OR HIDE?

Instead of going straight to the top, Miller and Wedell-Wedellsborg have a number of alternatives to consider.

Stealth sponsors are senior managers below the executive director level but who will have enough power to make progress and clear some roadblocks (but not all). The authors suggest a few rules in finding a sponsor. First, pick someone that you know well. This won't be about the idea, it's about your relationship. If you've already established trust with someone, it will be easier to recruit their support.

Consider what's in it for the potential sponsor. If your idea will be beneficial to them and/or their career, then they are more likely to support it than something that would damage them (e.g. by cannibalizing sales in their group).

As a prelude to getting them on board, you can test their position by asking their advice before you go all in and ask for their backing.

Stealth-testing means finding a way to gather evidence that the concept has value before it is put in front of senior management. The story of Post-it® Notes describes how, in the face of disinterest from marketing, some notes were created and distributed. When individuals got used to using them, they were redirected to ask for more from marketing. The real story might be slightly different but you can see this as one way of demonstrating true demand for a product or service.

You should be looking for ways to prove the value of the idea. Enthusiasm is to be expected from someone with a 'good' idea but convincing other people will require more than energy and some PowerPoint slides. You need to get as close to incontrovertible proof as can reasonably be done.

Stealth resourcing

This means finding ways to barter or negotiate the use of resources on the quiet. A lot of the time management's job is to avoid this happening. Management involves the best use of a finite set of resources and so having an 'off the books' activity going on is not an ideal situation. However, if you're the one with the good idea, it's in everyone's interests if you can get it through to successful launch. It depends which hat you're wearing as to whether this is a good thing or a bad thing.

One interesting idea beyond scavenging and doing barter deals for time and resources internally is to find external resources. Broadcaster TV 2 [http://tv2.dk/] in Denmark developed a stealth-resourced mobile content business by working with mobile operators who would benefit from, and therefore fund, the initiatives in this area.

Stealth branding

Miller and Wedell-Wedellsborg talk about providing a credible cover story that means you can invest the time in the 'secret' project – avoiding prying eyes and questions. Not so sure I'd always be happy about using this idea but I guess it can work.

The bottom line is that starting in stealth mode allows you to make substantial progress before 'going public' with the idea.

So when should you consider innovating in this fashion?

The researchers stress two questions to consider as you consider going to the top versus a stealthier approach to progressing the idea. You're essentially balancing these two risks.

What is the downside for the company? If you go stealth mode then what about ethical or legal issues. Could you be jeopardizing the company? The researchers don't mention it but also what happens if stealth is the wrong approach and it delays progressing the idea, or it remains starved of the necessary resources? In that case, choosing the stealth approach would be responsible for a failure.

What is the downside for you? If you get caught using the stealth approach are you going to be rewarded for showing initiative or kicked for misusing resources? That's a judgement call and the more you've used the 'stealth branding' approach, the deeper trouble you might be in when discovered.

So what are the big takeaways here?

That depends on your role and therefore your perspective on the situation.

- **Don't drive innovation underground.** Within an organization, I'd rather have a channel for people with ideas to exploit them. That means a structured innovation process and pipeline for ideas. I'd prefer it was easy for people to put their ideas into an 'official' process rather than hide what's going on. The researchers discuss Nick Leeson and other rogue traders who believed more in trying to achieve an end result than following an internal process. If you can make it easier for ideas and innovators to get support officially then you should have visibility of what is happening. Don't drive this stuff underground.
- **Make the right move.** As an individual with an idea, I'd be thinking very carefully about which approach to follow and what the consequences might be. What's the course of action that provides the best chance of ensuring this idea can and will deliver value for the business.

- **People fall in love with their own ideas all the time.** It's in your interest to back up any ideas you have with the evidence required to convince other people. Your judgement should be used to figure out if the back of an envelope is enough or if Nobel Prize winning is needed. You aim to do the minimum needed to go official. It's just that sometimes the minimum is actually a huge amount of work.

Source

Miller, Paddy & Wedell-Wedellsborg, Thomas, *Innovation as Usual: How to Help Your People Bring Great Ideas to Life* (Harvard Business Review Press, Boston, 2013)

See also

Chapter 34 – On the 'right' amount of innovation – considering the correct balance between different types of innovation for your organization.

Further reading

Cooper, Robert G., *Winning at New Products: Creating Value Through Innovation* (Basic Books, New York, 2011)

36 THERE ARE JUST THREE RULES

What choices should be made to ensure the best business performance?

They say that in theory, practice and theory are the same, but in practice they aren't!

The management world is full of lots of wisdom from academics and business people. However, one rule of thumb in terms of considering advice from entrepreneurs is have they succeeded twice? Living in Cambridge in the UK, I know and have worked with plenty of people who have been in the right place at the right time and been able to build a reasonable business once. However, the most extreme example of someone who perhaps was lucky rather than good managed to succeed once and then fail with the next ten ventures (and counting).

Truisms are easy to find in management thinking. Peters and Waterman in 1982 had the idea of 'sticking to your knitting' – in other words you do what you know and are good at. The core competence work a few years later was similar but focused on companies understanding their deep-lying abilities and finding new ways to leverage these rather than trying to develop new ones. However, the example companies quoted in the Peters and Waterman book *In Search of Excellence* are now mainly dead. This is not a fair stick to beat the book with as we're talking about something written more than 30 years ago, but it does suggest that understanding the long-term performance of businesses, and looking at bigger sets of companies, will increase the value of any findings.

There are some very interesting pieces of work where people have assessed significant numbers of companies. For example, David Sirota et al's book *The Enthusiastic Employee* has some important but simple things to say about motivation on the basis of a very large study. It's well worth reading.

In the context of strategy, one piece of outstanding work was carried out by two members of the consultants Deloitte – Michael E. Raynor and Mumtaz Ahmed. They summarized a very extensive piece of work in the *Harvard Business Review*. How does 25,000 companies sound as a basis for their research? That's what they looked at, finding companies that had traded on US stock exchanges between 1966 and 2010.

As a measure of performance, they used ROA (Return On Assets). Now that is not always a good measure in the short term as exceptional capital expenditure or temporary changes in the market or focus of the business will change the ROA. However, over a longer period of time it's a reasonable metric of business performance.

Now one obvious flaw would be to simply compare companies across all sectors. A railway company and a supermarket have extraordinarily different characteristics in terms of their assets, revenues, etc. ROA is therefore only a sensible comparison between companies in the same sector.

In putting their book together, the authors' reasoning was to find management thinking that has some deep justification rather than being the rationalization after the event of why business A or B happened to succeed.

So which companies were classed as doing well?

The pair categorized some companies as 'Miracle Workers'. These companies had been in the top 10 per cent of their respective sector/group often enough to suggest their performance was more than just luck. A second subset called the 'Long Runners' comprised those that were in the top 20 per cent to 40 per cent consistently enough to again assume luck didn't play a part.

They also identified companies they called 'Average Joes' to represent run-of-the-mill performance.

From the huge initial set of companies, they were able to define 174 companies as Miracle Workers and 170 as Long Runners.

Once they had identified these good performers, the next question was to understand the differences that resulted in superior results. To do this they considered nine market segments and one company from each category ('Miracle Worker', 'Long Runner' and 'Average Joe') within each of the segments.

At this point, more digging was required into the underlying businesses to try to understand how different elements in the overall performance were impacting the ROA figure. This ranged from asset turnover through to margins and detailed costs.

What did they learn?

You can imagine how much hard work went into formulating and testing ideas that turned out to be dead ends across such a big sample of companies.

However, they were eventually able to come up with some very simple and clear rules based around some choices in how companies compete.

As a general rule, the 'Miracle Workers' are more reliant on superior gross margins (revenues less the cost of goods sold) than on using lower costs to create better profitability. Not clear? Well they are generally able to obtain a higher gross margin on their products than competitors.

'Long Runners' typically are more reliant on an advantage in terms of the selling price than on the gross margin advantage of the 'Miracle Workers'.

The authors simplified the choices that a company can make and suggested it can compete on the basis of these two options. These were not arbitrary. They were identified as correlating closely with performance. Before explaining the findings further, let's understand the two fundamental choices:

'Nonprice' is their term for competing based on functionality, quality, brand image and other differentiators that do not relate to price.

Another positioning they termed 'Price'. This approach involves doing the minimum required for the market in terms of product/ service functionality, ease of use, etc.

The third implied positioning is a little like Michael Porter's 'stuck in the middle'. It's the highly undesirable situation where the company's thinking is clearly neither one thing nor the other.

So what did the authors discover? Let's look at the findings and how we might apply them.

SIMPLE RULES

Rule 1 – Better before cheaper

'Miracle Workers' tend to focus on non-price approaches. Okay you might be expecting something very complex here, but that's it. Rule 1 – the better business performers over the long term looked to provide better products and services rather than focusing on lower cost positions.

Rule 2 – Revenue before cost

The 'Miracle Workers' achieve better profits by outstripping the revenue of their competitors. They do this with higher prices or by achieving higher volumes.

As a concept, the linkage between higher prices and higher profits is obvious. However, we're talking about the majority of the 'Miracle Workers' that have been able to do this across a variety of different market segments – driving to find ways that they can charge more than their competition. A smaller percentage of the 'Miracle Workers' based their superior revenue generation on volume – reducing underlying costs through economies of scale.

I've heard it said there are three types of people in this world – those that understand maths and those that don't. Well there are three rules here... and the third kind of fits in with that joke.

Rule 3 – There are only two rules

That's pretty simple then isn't it.

So how do you apply the rules in practice? It seems a bit simple doesn't it?

In a perfect world, our analysis of the business environment, the actions of our competitors and the needs of our competitors is so clear and compelling that the company knows exactly what to do. Sadly, situations are often so complex that the way forward is unclear.

What these rules provide, and you can hardly forget them, are a couple of thoughts to bear in mind as you weigh up the evidence and options about different potential directions in front of you. The short-term drive to try to cost-save and shave ways back to improved profitability may yield attractive results in the short term. However, in the medium term the failures to invest increase the chance of killing a business as it is forced to adapt to market changes and competitive actions in a reactive way – rather than with good preparation ahead of time.

So what are the big takeaways here?

- **Don't try to cost-cut your way into the future.** Cost-cutting and optimizing operations is okay but not in isolation and certainly not as the only long-term strategic approach.
- **Satisfying short-term needs is good for earning bonuses and satisfying shareholders.** However, to ensure a company survives into the future, decisions need to be more forward thinking. How will this course of action impact on how we compete in a year... in two years ... in three years?

Source

Raynor, Michael & Ahmed, Mumtaz, *The Three Rules: How Exceptional Companies Think* (Portfolio, New York, 2013)

See also

Chapter 32 – A similarly profound and revelatory discussion. Simple rules based on large samples. Both Chapter 32 and this one should be considered very carefully.

Further reading

Sirota, David, Mischkind, Louis A. & Meltzer, Michael Irwin, *The Enthusiastic Employee* (FT/Prentice Hall, New Jersey, 2005)

37 A REPEATABLE BUSINESS MODEL?

A simple way to create a differentiated strategy?

As discussed earlier in Chapter 15, creating lasting differentiation is becoming more difficult, but Zook and Allen may have found a formula for doing it!

The work by Chris Zook and James Allen starts by restating that differentiation is the key element in creating differential advantage. It might be easy to dismiss the notion that success can be codified in this way, but their findings were based on research into 8,000 companies – working steadily to identify elements that create differentiation for them.

The first finding was that 80 per cent of the high-performing companies had a well-defined point (or points) of differentiation at the heart of their strategy. For example, they suggest Apple competes because of the combination of easy-to-use software, the integration of the iTunes and Apple Store ecosystem, design skills and simple product set.

Another finding is that the quality of the differentiation and execution is four times more important than the particular market in determining why a company achieves 'high performance'. That's pretty profound right? Direction and execution trump environment!

Over time, Zook and Allen suggest that success in maintaining differentiation can also create 'disbenefits', such as over-complexity. Differentiation through product proliferation will make it harder to achieve the same economies of scale as would be possible with a simpler product line-up. For example, at the time of their research, they counted only 60 main products from Apple. However, the need to match competitor products (e.g. the expanding size range of Android tablets) means that by late 2014, the number of variants of the iPad alone had risen to 56.

There are other drivers that make it harder to maintain a strong position. As a business grows, the 'distance' between management and those on the front line will get larger. Functions become more specialized and silo-like as the companies grow, and it can be hard to remember what you're good at and why you've succeeded. I often see larger companies, made up of multiple Strategic Business Units, where the strategy process has become little more than a summation of individual SBU budgets. These budgets are then tweaked centrally – normally meaning someone adds some extra on top of the targets and that's it. This doesn't happen in smaller, vibrant companies. This is why this research is so interesting as it really focuses on maintaining that sense of identity about who the company is and how it competes. If that latter point is kept front and centre in people's minds, you are more likely to consider how changes will worsen or enhance that differentiation.

Zook and Allen believe that the most successful companies achieve this success through a continual evolutionary process – updating the sources of differentiation to maintain their performance in the market.

There were some interesting findings along the way. Zook and Allen highlight the problem of understanding differentiation. Although 80 per cent of managers in their work suggested their company was differentiated, only 10 per cent of the customers agreed. Who is right? Well differentiation has to be in the mind of the customer – otherwise does it really exist? Easy answer. No it doesn't!

From their work, the team was able to identify 250 different attributes that contribute to differentiation. They were then able to group the attributes into three broad areas as shown in the following Differentiation Map.

The work indicated that the top performing companies created strategy around a number of sources of differentiation. These sources should ideally be complementary. That means that to

Portfolio Management and Finance	M&A, Joint Ventures and Partnering	Regulatory Management	Business Unit Strategy and Driving Priorities	HR Management and Culture

OPERATING CAPABILITIES

Supply Chain and Logistics	Production and Operations	Development and Innovation	Go-to-Market	Customer Relationships

PROPRIETARY ASSETS

Tangible Assets	Scale	Technology and IP	Brand	Tied Customer Network

BACK OFFICE → **CUSTOMER FACING**

Figure 37.1 A Differentiation Map

some extent one aspect will be reinforcing another and so on within the organization.

APPLYING THE THINKING

There are six steps that can be taken to apply this research.

1. The first is a fundamental questioning of what the actual sources of differentiation are. Ask everyone in the management team to identify their own view of what are the company's sources of differentiation. Ask them: What do our customers think are the key points of differentiation between us and competitors?
   - Why do we believe this? What's the evidence? Remember the mismatch mentioned earlier between the internal company view and customer opinions on whether a company is differentiated!
   - Are the sources of differentiation becoming stronger or waning? I'd add that you should probably also ask, how quickly are they changing, are they still relevant and are they under threat from new product/service configurations?
2. Ask people further down the organization what they think is the strategy. I do this all the time. You're likely to be depressed by the lack of understanding of what the organization is trying to achieve as you go deeper into the organization.

3. Write out the strategy on one page. This is an exercise to focus the mind on what is important. Does it centre on the sources of differentiation? Is it well-founded? Would all the different stakeholders agree?

4. Consider the last 20 projects or investments aimed at growth. Do these help explain the relative success or failure of the company during the period? Consider the way these activities strengthened or weakened existing differentiators or created new ones. If they didn't relate to key differentiators, then why were they carried out?

5. Try to convert the strategy into fundamental but simple principles that the business can get behind. These principles should help direct business operations from values down to behaviours that are needed to deliver these principles.

6. Reconsider the performance metrics you measure in the business. If you're using a balanced scorecard or other metrics scheme, are the sources of differentiation included? They are pretty fundamental to business success. What about how they are evolving? Do you measure them well enough to know what might need changing? If you identify changes are needed – are they carried out?

The Differentiation Map can be a useful tool in expressing where a company believes its sources of differentiation lie. With the 15 categories in the map, there are more than 5,000 combinations of key sources of differentiation. With a more detailed view, the researchers suggest the total number of combinations rises above 1 million. There is no silver bullet configuration that can be applied to any business that will work for it. Sorry, that would be too easy. But the map is a great tool for questioning where you are in terms of differentiation and forming agreement where there are conflicting views or a lack of clarity.

Another interesting exercise is to use the map to consider the positions of your direct competitors. Map where you think their points of differentiation are located in the Differentiation Map discussed earlier in the chapter. To add some further subtlety to the maps, you could comment on whether their sources of differentiation are growing, stable or waning. This will help you better understand the overall position for your business.

So what are the big takeaways here?

- **Ensure the sources of competitive advantage are at the heart of your strategy.** This should ideally be in ways that are self-reinforcing. Sounds easy? It won't be, but if this thinking is central to the strategic process and you ensure the organization understands how it competes, you are in with a better chance of it acting in a way that is consistent with maintaining its competitive advantages.
- **How do we compete?** That's an astonishingly useful question to ask and to flesh out. How do our customers believe we compete – why do they buy from us? Why do they buy from our competition? What is changing in those relationships? Ask those questions internally and of your customers. Explore them and challenge them fully. Rely more on what your customers say than your own internal viewpoints. Many companies fall in love with their own products and arguments. It only counts if the market does.
- **Nothing lasts forever.** Longevity is an increasingly rare thing in the business world. Nobody can rest on their laurels.

Source

Zook, Chris & Allen, James, *Repeatability: Build Enduring Businesses for a World of Constant Change* (Harvard Business Review Press, Boston, 2012)

See also

Chapter 28 – Talks about the concept of reinforcement of different aspects of the business model.

Chapter 17 – Provides some mechanisms to identify when your business model is in trouble.

Chapter 22 – Outlines approaches to building innovation into the business model.

Further reading

Lafley, A. G. & Martin, Roger L., *Playing to Win: How Strategy Really Works* (Harvard Business Review Press, Boston, 2013)

38 HOW TO ENSURE EMPLOYEES 'GET' STRATEGY

How and why, in terms of strategy, simple rules rule!

Simplicity is a great virtue. CEOs should have simple principles as they're easy to share and people understand them without difficulty. Strategy is the same. Ideally, you want everyone in the organization to understand the strategy and work in a way that is consistent with it. If your employees don't understand the strategy – how can they work in line with it?

Uncertainty leads to wavering and inconsistency.

We can agree that it's important but how do you actually ensure strategy is transmitted effectively throughout an organization?

Donald Sull and Kathleen Eisenhardt have written on this topic and cite some interesting experiments outlining the superiority of simplicity. They describe work by Iyengar and Lepper where shoppers were offered free samples of 6 types of jam: 40 per cent of shoppers had a look and 30 per cent bought some jam. With 24 types of jam on display, 60 per cent of shoppers stopped but only 3 per cent bought any.

In a similar vein, a study of the take-up of pension rights showed 75 per cent of employees took up the offer when faced with only two plans. This fell to 61 per cent when the number of funds rose into the tens.

We can infer that people can become paralysed by complexity.

Sull and Eisenhardt have been looking at the area of the dissemination of strategy for more than a decade and have an understanding of why simple rules are more effective and how to define them.

They have created some simple rules... for generating simple rules. It's rather elegant.

Set corporate objectives

Consider, what are you trying to do in terms of profit, growth, etc.?

I'd suggest that thinking about the product, profit and people propositions might be helpful to flesh out this definition.

Identify a bottleneck that is in the way of meeting the strategic objectives

The bottleneck in this case refers to the place or places where achieving your objective is being thwarted (as it is beyond the resources you have at your disposal). You're looking for the biggest gaps – which should equate to the biggest potential wins.

The bottleneck must relate to a critical problem in meeting part or all of a strategic objective or you'd be looking at something more minor than you should in this approach.

The bottleneck needs to be well defined and relatively focused. It can't be a general problem such as 'training' or 'lack of finance'. If it is that fuzzy, you'd struggle to come up with a specific way to improve it.

Then you ask where/how you could change the process to help improve the situation by putting in place new rules.

You're looking for a place or a couple of places where new rules will have the most impact.

The authors explain how one organization (IDEO) was having ideas pushed through too quickly by customers. This meant they were going too quickly through to prototype. When an immature or inappropriate idea gets to that stage, you have spent more money and used up scarce resources on something that will not actually become a product. They recognized that more time brainstorming and thinking would enable the firm to generate better ideas. In this case, brainstorming was the strategic bottleneck. The simple rules derived to counteract this problem were put on the conference room walls to keep them at the top of people's thinking. 'Defer judgement.' 'Encourage wild ideas.' 'Go for quantity.' See? Simple rules!

Create simple rules to manage the bottlenecks

What is the history of that process – what worked, what didn't? You're looking to get evidence and wisdom out of available data, rather than suffering from any personal bias or hunches from your management team. If you look into what's gone on previously, you may find counterintuitive patterns that you can use for the future.

Much of this book is based on this process. Consider situations, create hypotheses and test them. Approve, revise or reject the hypotheses at the end of the tests.

SPREADING THE WORD

Charles Galunic, a professor of leadership at INSEAD, has written with Immanuel Hermreck about why the concept of strategy cascading down into an organization fails. They looked through 60,000 employee responses from a 300-company global corporation to try to understand the underlying conditions that would support the strategy being embedded. Interestingly, factors like longevity in the company did not strongly correlate with a person being familiar with the strategy.

They were able to come up with three problems that mean the strategy cascading down into the organization can be ineffective.

- Only senior management is able to give strategic communication sufficient weight. Employees want to hear these messages from the senior team (and that works better in embedding the strategic thinking down into the organization).

- The trade-offs involved in strategy are better accepted when put in the wider picture painted by a senior management team, than when filtered by various layers of management and self-interest.
- The process of the message passing down the organization inevitably leads to it being modified and lost in translation.

The rules that are set need to come from the right people and be sufficiently robust

As with a project that aims to change the way that an organization operates, you want the people defining a rule to be the ones that will be operating it. They will know the bottleneck and associated problems the best. So they should be best placed to craft the rule(s) to get around it.

The rules should be concrete. The film *Moneyball* describes the system used by the Oakland Athletics' general manager to select players. It was grounded in baseball statistics, which were interpreted to create rules about which players would be selected (and which ones would not).

Case study: Failure to communicate in a financial services group

I asked a set of regional managers how the meeting with the new CEO had gone. It was their first chance to meet the new guy and I was interested to see what clarity this would provide on the strategy. After a few nods, one RM explained that he still didn't understand the strategy. He'd heard the words from the CEO but the language used was so flowery and complex that he'd tuned out and couldn't really pass on the strategy. Lesson one underlined then. Keep the language simple as well as the message or you risk losing some of the audience, or even antagonizing them.

My favourite topic with the same group was a series of individual projects that were being undertaken as part of a change initiative. The only problem was that the topics of these projects were a secret. None of the regional managers knew more than a couple of the projects that were underway so every time they had an idea for something to do within the organization, they were instantly demotivated by the thought that someone else might be doing the same project already.

If your senior management teams don't understand the strategy and can't act without fear of wasting their efforts, then things have room to improve, to say the least.

So what are the big takeaways here?

- **Ensure senior management is communicating the strategy directly.** This will reduce mistranslations and bias effects from diminishing the understanding of the strategy further down the organization.
- **Communicate, communicate, communicate.** The learning from change projects says this since you need to ensure people have got the message and understand it clearly. To that end, make sure the message is easy to understand and consistent. You can never overestimate how mangled even the simplest message can become.

Sources

Galunic, C. & Hermreck, I., 'How to Help Employees "Get" Strategy', *Harvard Business Review*, December 2012

Sull, Donald & Eisenhardt, Kathleen M., *Simple Rules for a Complex World* (Houghton Mifflin Harcourt, Boston, 2015

See also

Chapters 1 and 2 – Underline how important it is to both have a strategy and also ensure it is clearly understood throughout the organization.

Using the Balanced Scorecard to align what you do with what you are trying to achieve

If you want to scare yourself, remember my suggestion to ask people in a business what they think the strategy is. Typically they will struggle. If there is an explicit strategy, you can ask what are the projects and programmes that underpin a particular aspect of the strategy. If there is nothing that can be pinpointed, then you can be pretty sure that aspect is not going to succeed.

As mentioned previously, what you're looking for is that people and groups are acting in a way that is consistent with the strategy. If not then you have problems. You need a tight connection between the strategy and supporting objectives down to actions – and you ensure you're doing the important things by measuring their progress.

In the early 1990s a number of research programmes were looking at measurement of performance in businesses. This covered both more traditional financial measures as well as non-financial ones.

What can derail this link, apart from ignorance of the strategic direction, is having the wrong metrics in place. People keen to keep their job, earn the bonus, get a pay rise or be promoted are likely to focus on how their performance is measured. If that measurement is not consistent with the strategy then don't be surprised if you get the wrong results.

One approach to solving the conundrum of how to get what you expect in relation to the strategy, is the Balanced Scorecard (BSC). Although various researchers were publishing in this area, broader interest in linking metrics to strategic choices was ignited by publication of Robert Kaplan and David Norton's book *The Balanced Scorecard*.

When used well, it's a great tool for connecting strategy to day-to-day actions. Unfortunately, when used badly it gives the impression that a company is running a tight ship while potentially glossing over serious issues.

The key is the linkage between strategy and things that are relevant and important.

The scorecard evolved in three flavours.

The first versions evolved around measurements in four areas – Financial, Processes, Customers, and Learning and Growth. The suggestion is that you start from the business mission/vision.

That can be tricky where a company's mission is very terse or is a dressed-up marketing message that hides the real intent of the business. Disney's mission is 'To make people happy'. I'd suggest that is so broad that it doesn't really help in the breakdown of day-to-day actions. So let's work forward from a well-articulated, up-to-date strategy that accurately reflects the business's current and future situation.

However, if we assume the strategy has been developed correctly, the key is to identify critical success factors for the business that relate to these different areas, prioritize them and then add the most important to the scorecard with appropriate targets.

In Figure 39.1 you can see that each objective is linked to a particular measurement with a target and also a space to show which initiatives/projects/programmes are aiming to improve performance against that metric.

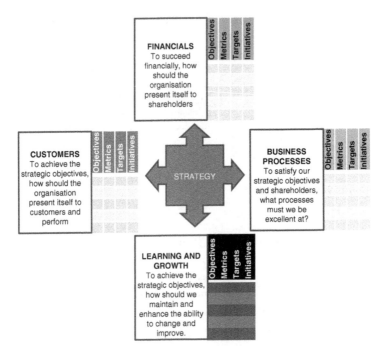

Figure 39.1 The Balanced Scorecard

As you can imagine, if you get this right this could be a good way of focusing attention in the business. However, a concern was that this approach did not work as easily across more complex organizational designs (multiple divisions, conglomerates, etc.).

The second approach tried to strengthen the link with strategy through the creation of 'Strategy Maps'.

This simple example suggests that enhancing the skills in the business may in turn improve the speed and quality of processes, improving delivery time, keeping customers happier and leading on to better returns for the business.

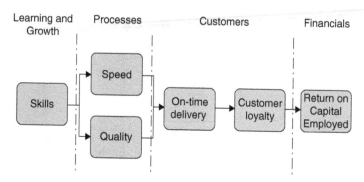

Figure 39.2 An example strategy map

The example below shows the Strategy Map for a low-cost airline (as shown in Chapter 31) trying to improve the utilization of its main assets (the planes) by turning them around more quickly. It starts with the grounds crews and leads to, if all the links hold true, more profit.

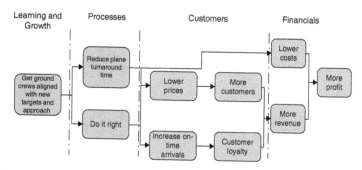

Figure 39.3 A strategy map for a low-cost airline

A strategy map enables people to consider the cause and effect of different elements and then critique and improve the map, meaning better metrics are likely to be selected.

The latest methodology for a balanced scorecard works the end point of any strategic actions first. It specifies where the company will be using a Destination Statement that defines 'success' for the company in a couple of pages. The statement contains perspectives in categories from the original ones and which now cover expectations relating to organization/culture, financial (including stakeholders), customer/external relationships and processes/activities.

A second element is a modified version of the strategy map that is called the Strategic Linkage Model. This incorporates the key 12 to 24 objectives that support the successful execution of the strategy and are either activities or outcomes. Again the logical path through the model should be clear to illustrate how the organization will achieve its overall goals by following the different steps.

LINKING STRATEGY TO OBJECTIVES

First, you need to understand the strategy for your organization and it has to be as good as you can do with what you know today. If your business hasn't got that right then stop now... go do that and only then think about the Balanced Scorecard approach. Otherwise, you'll almost certainly be measuring the wrong things and perhaps fondly imagining that things are going well.

To figure out what to measure, the Balanced Scorecard approach says you should try to identify the most important goals supporting delivery of the strategy.

You won't always be able to get to these directly so the first step is to define the Destination Statement. A good way to build this is to start to identify what that 'success' looks like and then categorize objectives for achieving the success into the different categories – organization/culture, financial (including stakeholders), customer/external relationships and processes/activities.

The right people need to carry out this exercise. It's important to have input from across the organization or you may find the results are skewed or miss important areas.

Objective	Candidate critical success factors
Grow to market share of 30 per cent in territory A	Gain new customers Increase competitiveness versus other local providers
Achieve supply in 16 hours for 90 per cent of the product range	Sustain successful relationships with distribution channel
Expand product range to attract more customers	Source new products
Reach and then maintain a customer satisfaction rate of at least 97 per cent	Retain staff and keep up customer-focused training
Extend product range to attract new products and customers	Secure financing for expansion

Figure 39.4 Objectives and potential Critical Success Factors (CSFs)

Figure 39.4 shows some possible Critical Success Factors. Now as you look down that list, the first thing that comes to mind is that some may relate to major contributions to the organization while others are relatively unimportant.

When you create your list, each CSF should be prioritized for how well they really relate to achieving the strategy and also their relevance across more than one business unit (in more complex organizations). Doing this will illustrate if you are missing objectives in one particular area. The outcome should be a list across the four categories of between 12 and 24 objectives that support the Destination Statement.

For each objective that makes it into that final list of between 12 and 24, there are metrics that will tell you whether you are succeeding or not. These metrics need to be identified but also the target performance level they relate to. There's no point measuring something if you don't know what you're aiming at.

At the end of the exercise, you should have a table of the metrics and targets divided into the four business areas.

As with many exercises of this type, if you don't do anything with that table then you might as well not have bothered creating it.

The next stage is to review current initiatives in the business and create new ones if necessary that will help deliver against the targets, or stop ones that you think are not contributing to getting to the destination defined in the statement.

At the end, if you'd done it right, you should have the right things to measure, to achieve the most important objectives in reaching your strategic targets. That wouldn't be too bad would it?

So what are the big takeaways here?

- **Develop a great destination statement first.** If you can't do that everything else will be wasted. Creating a Strategic Linkages Model will help enormously.
- **Ask if the objectives and critical success factors relate to what you have to do to succeed.** Or have you simply listed a 'nice to have'? Keep challenging them in this way to ensure you get the most relevant list you can. In trying to understand the value of each objective, try to see what else it affects in the strategic linkage model.
- **It's not always about perfecting things in a business.** The better you do things the more it may cost and the more effort it may take to get there. Accept that for some things, good enough is going to be good enough.

Source

Kaplan, Robert S. & Norton, David P., *The Balanced Scorecard* (Harvard Business Review Press, Boston, 1996)

See also

Chapter 31 – Shows how some of the Balanced Scorecard thinking can be integrated into getting the business model right.

Further reading

Kaplan, R. S. & Norton, D. P., 'How to implement a new strategy without disrupting your organization', *Harvard Business Review*, March 2006

40 CONSIDERING AN END-TO-END APPROACH

A journey through one strategic evaluation approach

The book shows plenty of fragments of the strategic process. I think it's also interesting to look at one overarching approach and see how it fits different elements together.

The book includes a few classic pieces of thinking like the Five Forces Model from Michael Porter, but Professor Michael Jacobides has suggested that in today's more turbulent world, that approach may even be actively misleading!

It won't be one size fits all as common sense and, if you want any reinforcement of that fact, Chapter 20 will tell you.

So let's look at The Five-Step Strategy Model and then how that is implemented.

A. G. Lafley and Roger Martin have looked at the strategic intent of a wide variety of companies as well as bringing their own unique combined view on management. Lafley is a former CEO of Procter & Gamble while Martin was previously dean at the Rotman School of Management. Their book, *Playing to Win: How Strategy Really Works*, is a very good read.

They don't try to dress up strategy as something complicated or impenetrable. Instead, they boil it down to a simple set of questions that create choices for an organization. In turn, the choices should provide a unique positioning for the organization in its sector. Although Chapter 15 suggests that sustainable competitive advantage may be increasingly elusive, Lafley and Martin believe your choices should be aiming to find it if possible, as well as superior value creation and appropriation compared to the competition.

They developed this Five-Step Strategy Model to structure the questions that an organization should look to answer. However, let's also complement it with a couple of ideas from Kim and Mauborgne's *Blue Ocean Strategy* (see Chapter 30).

What is your winning aspiration? Why do you exist? What are you trying to achieve? If you genuinely can't win, then play somewhere else or stop playing.

Where will you play? Choose your battles. In which industries, segments, geographies, etc. can you achieve the above aspiration? This has to be considered in parallel with the next question about how you can win. Linking these two together is important in finding a strong position for the organization. Bear in mind that the competitive environment may be very turbulent and your choices need to consider this.

How will you win? Given the aspiration and the places you've chosen to play, how will you win? What will your competitive advantage be? From Blue Ocean thinking, we can expand this to include definitions of:

- A value proposition that attracts buyers
- A profit proposition that means the company makes money from the value proposition
- A people proposition that encourages the right behaviour from those within the company to deliver the strategy. This will impact how well the company executes.

What capabilities must be in place? The resources and capabilities the organization needs to succeed in the way outlined in the previous steps.

What management systems are required? This refers to the systems and measures that support the organizational capabilities used to win in the chosen fashion and in the selected playing field.

In a similar vein, you have Donald C. Hambrick and James W. Fredrickson with their Strategy Diamond (shown below).

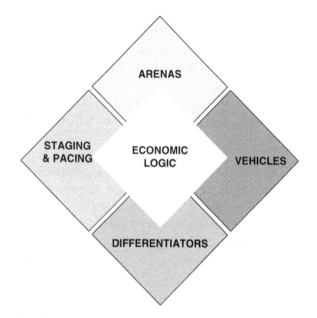

Figure 40.1 Strategy Diamond (Donald C. Hambrick and James W. Fredrickson). Reprinted by permission *The Academy of Management Executive*, Vol. 15 No. 4 pp 48–59. Copyright © 2001

Arenas refers to where you will compete, with which approaches to value creation, which technologies, etc. Vehicles are about the ventures, acquisitions, partnerships and JVs you may use to help get you to your objectives. Staging and Pacing describes the speed you will go at and the step size you will take on the way.

The Economic Logic in the centre is similar to the idea of a profit proposition. It is about how the company will make a profit – cost leadership strategy, premium pricing, economies of scale...

WALKING IT THROUGH

To support creating a good strategy, Lafley and Martin also define a simple but structured approach.

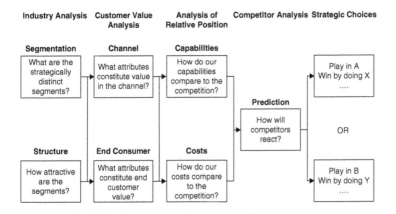

Figure 40.2 Lafley and Martin's strategy approach model

Reprinted by permission of Harvard Business Review Press. *From Playing to Win: How Strategy Really Works* by Lafley, A. G. & Martin, Roger L. 2013. Copyright © 2013 by Harvard Business Publishing; all rights reserved

The overall structure in the diagram leads a company's thinking from analysing the industry, considering what customers value and then on to understanding the competitive position and likely competitive reactions. This delivers a number of strategic choices that should respond to the questions raised earlier in the chapter.

Let's look at some of the elements in that work flow that may be less obvious from their titles.

Channel. Remember the question is always what value can be created and then how is it divided up. In the UK insurance markets, aggregators like Moneysupermarket and Gocompare have established such power that they can charge a finder's or referral fee to insurers on car insurance that is between £45 and £50. That's astonishing and most people I've asked imagine the aggregator's business model is based on wafer-thin margins.

End Consumer Value. This is an interesting one as we are in the era of big data driving customer information. The UK retailer Tesco relies on dunnhumby with its 40+ petabytes of data helping it to understand customer behaviour. However, you really need to engage with customers to understand what they value – e.g. face-to-face discussions, observations of them shopping, etc.

The authors also offer a few points to remember when working with this strategy logic flow as follows:

- Make sure you thoroughly consider each of the four dimensions that link to defining potential strategic choices
- Ensure you look beyond the current competitive situation – or quite simply you'll miss the more dynamic moves and opportunities that exist
- Drill down in seemingly unattractive industries to find attractive segments and/or find ways to change the rules of the game
- Watch out if either the channel or the end consumer value equation are unattractive for those participants. If either are unattractive, you risk losing your channel, the consumer or both
- The value in the channel or for the consumer needs to be figured out. But remember, those two players won't necessarily be able or willing to tell you
- Think about the full range of competitive reactions and the circumstances under which they may block your success. I'd add – don't assume they will respond in a logical fashion. Ego and fear as well as greed are strong motivators and sometimes your competitors will do the dumb thing you didn't expect.

So what are the big takeaways here?

- **This approach is a complement to other approaches.** Integrate these questions and the strategy workflow with whichever models you think are appropriate.
- **Check your thinking at every step.** Do we believe that what we are saying is possible? How can competitors stop us? What would have to happen for this to fail? What has to happen for us to succeed?
- **Think about the right things.** Lots of analysis is good but beware of static thinking about the competitive situation. See the bigger picture and consider all the players and all the moves they can make.

Sources

Hambrick, Donald C. & Fredrickson, James W. (2001), 'Are you sure you have a strategy?', *The Academy of Management Executive*, Vol. 15 No. 4 pp 48–59

Lafley, A. G. & Martin, Roger L., *Playing to Win: How Strategy Really Works* (Harvard Business Review Press, Boston, 2013)

McKinsey Quarterly. 2014 Issue 3 p 38–51

See also

Chapter 15 – Discusses how a sustainable competitive advantage is harder to attain.

Chapter 18 – Shows how classic strategic thinking needs to be extended to relate to the modern realities in business.

Further reading

Kim, W. Chan & Mauborgne, Renée, *Blue Ocean Strategy: How to Create Uncontested Market Space and Make the Competition Irrelevant* (Harvard Business School Publishing, Boston, 2005)

INDEX